HAUNTED FENTON

HAUNTED FENTON

BRENDA HASSE

Published by Haunted America
A Division of The History Press
Charleston, SC
www.historypress.com

Front cover: A.J. Phillips Fenton Museum. *Brenda Hasse.*
Back cover: Robert Wright, funeral director. *Fenton Historical Society.*

First published 2023

Manufactured in the United States

ISBN 9781467154093

Library of Congress Control Number: 2023932349

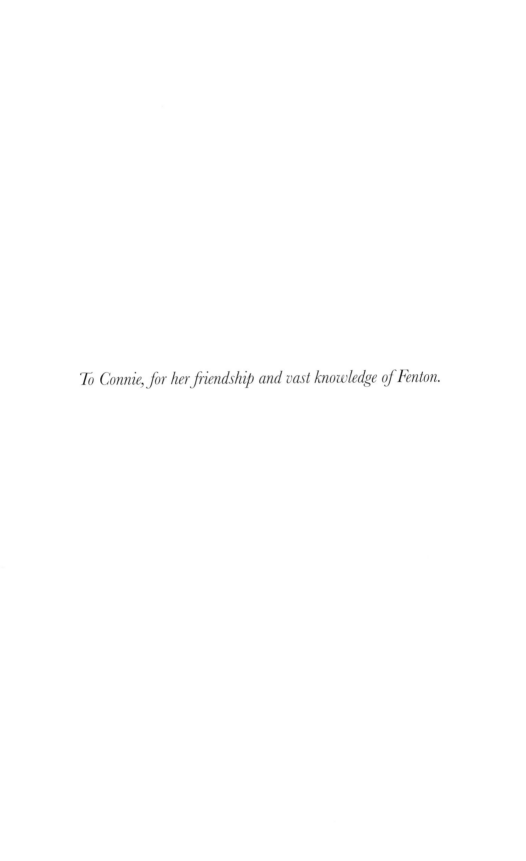

To Connie, for her friendship and vast knowledge of Fenton.

CONTENTS

CONTENTS

ACKNOWLEDGEMENTS

Thank you to Connie, Mickey and Kim, volunteers with the Fenton Historical Society, for sharing their extensive knowledge of Fenton's historical past. Their ability to swiftly research the history of Dibbleville, Fentonville and Fenton and find stories of interest is truly remarkable.

The society's vast library began when photographs and documents were gathered during the society's bicentennial year, 1934. Charles Damon identified the significance and importance of preserving such information, capturing the snapshot of the past, and is credited as the Fenton Historical Society's founder. The Fenton Historical Society's library is deep, thorough, and well-organized, with many photographs, articles, maps, books, yellowed and crumbling newspapers from the many publications that were produced over the years and historical records. It is continuously being updated as old photographs and documents are discovered. The volunteers of the Fenton Historical Society generously accommodated my requests and were willing to grant me access to their library of history within the A.J. Phillips Fenton Museum. The help and time invested by the society's volunteers in finding material for *Haunted Fenton* is truly appreciated.

Thank you to the residents and employees who live and work in the historic city of Fenton. I appreciate you stepping forward and sharing your stories of the hauntings you have and are experiencing in your homes and business establishments.

Mostly, thank you to the spirits who gently remind us of the city's past and continue to coexist among us.

Introduction

Imagine the day in 1834 when Clark Dibble stumbled onto an unsold parcel of land with rolling hills, fertile soil and a rippling stream that could be used as a source of drinking water and as a power source for a mill. The only other inhabitants of the land at that time were wild animals and a few indigenous Natives who used the area as a hunting ground.

After Dibble purchased the parcel, settlers converged on the community and built log cabins. Mills were constructed to produce lumber and food. As the population grew to establish a village, plank sidewalks were laid before retail shops. Streetlamps evolved from kerosine or oil to gas, requiring a lamplighter to set them aflame at night. The *clip-clop* of horses' hoofs on the dirt streets would echo throughout the bustling town, announcing someone's arrival. When the track of the railroad system was laid just north of the business district, the secret of quaint Fentonville was exposed, and the community experienced a boom in its population.

Established long ago, today's city of Fenton reflects its past. Still considered a small city, its current businesses continue to evolve and flourish, visitors travel from afar to eat in its renowned restaurants, and its citizens enjoys community events and gatherings.

The deceased residents from the budding years of Dibbleville and Fentonville slumber peacefully in the graves of Old Prospect Hill, located in the northeast corner of Oakwood Cemetery. Many of these citizens made their marks in history, while others remain unknown. Yet whatever their contribution, they helped make the lovely city what it is today. Visiting

Left: Old Prospect Hill marker. *Brenda Hasse*.

Below: Robert Wright, funeral director. *Fenton Historical Society*.

Old Prospect Hill is quietly eerie. Walking among the headstones, one may notice some of them are cracked, tilted and in need of repair or cleaning. Some of the plots are unmarked, or maybe the headstone is buried beneath the grass. Time has progressed, and some of the dead have been forgotten.

However, present-day residents and visitors to Fenton question if the dead are truly at rest. Do those who are no longer with us continue to exist in a dimension where they remain unseen? Those who reside in or around the city or visit one of its historic buildings often report unexplainable happenings. Some people claim to see dark shadow figures in their peripheral vision, hear disembodied voices, are touched by something they cannot see, witness objects moving on their own accord, hear heavy footsteps when alone in a building, and smell the fragrance of a pipe, cigar, or pungent perfume when others aren't around. However, others experience nothing at all.

Perhaps the past plays a part in our present. For example, in the heart of Fenton's historic district, two smaller establishments located at 108 and 407 South Leroy Street were previously offices of undertakers. The building at 115 West Shiawassee Avenue, built in 1920, was once a funeral home. Establishments such as these have a reputation of housing lost souls. It is rumored that those who work or visit these buildings experience a creepy feeling or may hear a disembodied child's laughter coming from behind them. Is it a figment of their imagination? For Fenton's residents who live in historic or older houses, they are aware of the time when the elderly, injured, and ill were not taken to a hospital to die. Instead, these poor souls gasped their last breaths and passed away in their homes. Are the restless spirits lost, trapped in limbo, or are they confused and uncertain of where to go? Do they not understand they are dead? Could they possibly be waiting for someone to join them? Do they have unfinished business that is keeping them earthbound? Or is there an unexplained scientific reason why our physical and the unseen nonphysical worlds coexist?

Many people choose to keep any strange happenings they experience to themselves or simply overlook them. Do they fear others may think they are not in their right mind? Do they think they will not be believed? Or do they have difficulty believing what they experienced themselves? The city of Fenton invites you to step into its historic community and discover if their spirits are truly at rest.

THE HISTORY OF FENTON

In 1834, Clark Dibble traveled from Pontiac toward Grumlaw; today, we know the settlement as Grand Blanc. He mistakenly followed the White Lake Trail and stumbled upon an unclaimed forty-acre parcel nestled in the center of five Native trails. Dibble was enchanted with the rich land and its water source (the Shiawassee River) and rolling hills. He filed a claim with the United States government in April 1834, paying $1.25 per acre. Dibble's claimed land encompassed Robert Street (Silver Lake Road) to South Street (South Holly Road) and East Street to West Street. He called the budding settlement Dibbleville before traveling north to Grumlaw to convince some of that community's settlers to relocate to his claimed parcel. The Dustin Cheney family arrived first and built a log cabin, shingled with elm bark, at the northwest corner of Adelaide Street and Shiawassee Avenue, the current location of A.J. Phillips's historic house. Soon to follow was Dibble, John Galloway and Loren Riggs.

Dibble built a one-room log cabin on the northeast side of the Shiawassee River for his family to reside in. Today, its former location in Millpond Park is signified with a marker. As travelers arrived in Dibbleville and stopped for the night, Clark welcomed them. He divided his home in half by rigging a blanket over a rope, and he offered his guests a place to sleep for the night. His family, including his wife and several small children, slept on one side of the room and his guests on the other.

With a handful of families making Dibbleville their home, Dibble knew other settlers would soon arrive. He built a dam and sawmill, powered by the rotation of an undershot waterwheel, to produce lumber that same year. In a few years, more than six hundred settlers had arrived. At that time, it took one man ten days to build a log cabin.

In 1836, Judge Daniel LeRoy recognized the importance of the location of Dibbleville. He predicted a railroad would run through the settlement someday and expand commerce in the area. He recommended his son, Robert LeRoy, and friend William M. Fenton, a brilliant young lawyer, travel to the small settlement. The two men, partners in selling goods, went to Dibbleville, agreed it was an excellent location and purchased it from Dibble in late 1836. Benjamin Rockwell, Fenton's brother-in-law, purchased one-third of the investment.

Since the trio no longer wanted the budding village to be known as Dibbleville, they decided on August 24, 1837, to let a game of cards determine who would have the privilege of renaming the settlement. Seven cards are rumored to have been dealt to each man. Fenton, who had the highest hand, a pair of queens and a pair of aces, won the right to call the settlement after himself. He named it Fentonville. LeRoy held the second-highest hand. Today, the town's main street bears his name, although it has been misprinted as Leroy

Street. Rockwell, who had the lowest hand, lent his name to a prominent residential street in town. Other streets were named after the men's wives and daughters. Some believe the famous poker game was played in the house at 609 South Leroy Street, which dates to 1837, while others think it may have been played in the Riggs Hotel. The Riggs Hotel was located approximately where the A.J. Phillips Fenton Museum is today. The Riggs Hotel was also built in 1837. One of the first buildings constructed by Mr. and Mrs. Fenton was located at the southwest corner of Adelaide Street and Shiawassee Avenue. The couple boarded up to thirty mechanics and builders there until the hotel was completed. In a short time, a second one-blade mill, gristmill, tavern and general store were added to

Dibbleville marker. *Brenda Hasse.*

The Game, depicting the famous game of poker that determined the city's name. *Brenda Hasse*.

The house where the poker game may have been played. *Fenton Historical Society*.

Fentonville. Other than by horseback or wagon, the stagecoach was the main mode of transportation, and Fentonville quickly became a stop. It was known as stop number seven (No. VII). Stop number six became the name of a city that exists today (No. VI is now known as Novi). For twenty years, most of the town's main gathering areas were located in the town square. William Fenton donated the land, which was triangular in shape. It is called Freedom Park today. Fentonville's name was changed to Fenton when it was incorporated in 1863. However, it was still referred to as Fentonville until 1886.

What happened to Clark Dibble? He purchased eighty acres in 1839 and moved to the area of White Lake Road and the U.S. 23 expressway with the intention of establishing a new settlement called Dibble. He built a tavern on what was known as the Trans-Michigan Turnpike and sold firewater to Natives and other passing travelers in the area. The Natives gave him the nickname "Cockawaisaw," which referred to the wind. While clearing the land of trees on June 22, 1842, Dibble's dog was in the way of a falling tree he had just cut. He rushed to push his dog out of the way. Although Dibble was successful in saving his dog, the tree fell on him, causing fatal injuries to which he succumbed. Dibble was buried in Old Prospect Hill, a section of Oakwood Cemetery. He died at the age of thirty-nine.

THE LOST CHILD

Settlers arriving in Michigan followed several Native trails and discovered unclaimed parcels of land. Today, we know these trails by other names. The best-known of these trails was the Saginaw Trail. We know it as Woodward Avenue, and it became the first paved road in the United States. The Shiawassee Trail crossed north of Walled Lake and Milford and down the valley along White Lake Road into Livingston County. The Grand River Trail went through Byron toward Lansing. In the early 1800s, fur traders used the Shiawassee River for trading. Trading posts were established on the Flint River, where furs were sold. Many Native villages and encampments were dotted in at to the rivers. Along the Shiawassee River were small encampments or villages of Sauk Natives who took advantage of the hunting and fishing available in the area. They held the lakes and waterways in reverence, making the north bank of Little Mud Lake (Crane Lake) their burial ground, where those who lay in rest could face the setting sun. The Objibwas and Ottawas, wanting to take advantage of the Sauk's hunting grounds, joined forces to overthrow the Sauk in several ruthless massacres and conquered their territory. As the migration brought more settlers into Michigan, the Natives moved out of the area. One such Native, Chief Fisher, refused to leave. He was easily recognizable with his ever-present top hat on his head. He was described as a brazen man who welcomed the settlers, and they welcomed him. His tribe lived on Lake Copneconic.

When Clark Dibble filed his claim on the forty-acre parcel that became Dibbleville, small settlements of Natives existed in the area. He then went to Grumlaw and convinced others to settle on his purchased land. One of the first settlers was the Dustin Cheney family. They built a log cabin on the northwest corner of West Shiawassee Avenue and Adelaide Street. Even though they brought supplies with them, their meals mostly consisted of venison, fish, buckwheat flapjacks and whatever else they could find growing naturally on the land and harvest. Their son Harrison was the first white baby born in the settlement. Before long, the Riggs and Galloway families joined the settlement. Dibble built a one-room log cabin and a sawmill on Millpond. His mill produced lumber for settlers to construct their homes. As word spread of the new settlement, Dibbleville's population began to grow.

Longing to provide for her large family, Abagail Cheney took two of her older children with her to find a suitable place to plant corn. Little Louisa, age three, wanted to go along on the adventure, but her mother told her to go inside the cabin and wait for her return. With her two children in tow, Abigail Cheney stepped into the wilderness—so did inquisitive Louisa but in a different direction. Louisa wandered in the wilderness and quickly lost her way. When Abigail returned to the cabin, she discovered her three-year-old daughter was missing. She and her other children searched the area for little Louisa but came up empty handed. A cry went up for, "Lost child! Lost child!" Before long, able-bodied men came from Grumlaw (Grand Blanc), Groveland, Holly, and White Lake to search for the child. They gathered in the town square (Freedom Park) and assigned each man an area to search. Abigail's husband, Dustin, joined the search as well. Unfortunately, no one discovered the whereabouts of little Louisa by nightfall. As her other children slept soundly that night, Abigail paced the dirt floor of her cabin. She wrapped her shawl around her shoulders and stepped outside in the hopes of hearing her daughter's cry for help. Knowing there were predatory animals in the area, she feared they would harm Louisa. Abigail stood silently and scanned the darkness. She wondered if her daughter was still alive.

For three days and three nights, little Louisa wandered the wilderness. Her body became riddled with itchy bumps from mosquito bites. She ate berries to appease her grumbling stomach and sipped water from puddles. Weak and tired, she laid on the ground and fell asleep. Those in the small community continued to search and pray for the child's safe return.

After working at Dibble's sawmill all day, Mr. Winchell was troubled by the news that the child was still missing after three days. After his workday ended, he spent several hours looking for little Louisa. He collapsed, nearly exhausted, into bed at midnight. He woke at two o'clock in the morning and recalled a dream he had about the lost child and the exact location in which to find her. He rose from bed, put on his hat, and went to the location. There, he found the three-year-old on the ground near the present-day location of Oakwood Cemetery. Winchell picked up the sleeping child and carried her home. Little Louisa was weak, exhausted from fright and lack of food. It took several weeks for the child to recover.

Once she became of age, Louisa M. Cheney married Galen T. Johnson. She died on September 30, 1863, at the age of thirty-four years, eleven months, and ten days. She was buried in plot 112 of Old Prospect Hill in Oakwood Cemetery.

COLONEL
WILLIAM MATTHEW FENTON

William Matthew Fenton was born on December 19, 1808. At a very young age, some described him as a boy who was at the top of his class, and he graduated from Hamilton College. Within a year's time, he sailed from Charleston, South Carolina, as a common sailor. After four years of sailing, he left his seafaring lifestyle, partnered with a merchantman, and was offered the captaincy of a vessel, which he declined. He married Adelaide S. Birdsall in April 1835. She was the daughter of Judge James Birdsall of Norwich, New York. Three months later, the couple settled in Pontiac, Michigan, where Fenton began a mercantile business with Robert LeRoy.

In 1836, Fenton, along with LeRoy, purchased Dibbleville from Clark Dibble. Fenton set up his mercantile business and invested in real estate and milling. He began to educate himself in law and was admitted to the bar in 1842. In 1844, he was the Democratic candidate for representation in the state legislature. He was defeated. Two years later, he was elected to the state senate, representing the counties of Genesee, Livingston, Macomb, and Oakland. While serving, he established the Institute for the Deaf, the Dumb, and the Blind in Flint. He was elected lieutenant governor in 1848 and was reelected to the office in 1850. He and his family moved to Flint in 1852. That same year, he was appointed register of the land office by President Pearce. He remained in that position until the land office was moved to Saginaw. He and his family traveled to Europe in 1856. In 1858, he was elected mayor of Flint. He is remembered for his ability and judgement

Cɔʟ. WM. M. FENTON
1808– 1871

Colonel William Matthew Fenton.
Fenton Historical Society.

in serving for the good of the city and all public interest he represented.

When the Civil War began, Fenton was a patriot who rose above political lines. When the first party of fighting men were called into duty, Fenton telegraphed Governor Blair offering $5,000 of his own money to supply the men with the proper equipment to go into battle. In early 1861, he was given the rank of major of the Seventh Michigan Infantry, but before the group was mustered, Governor Blair gave Fenton the rank of colonel of the Eighth Infantry. Fenton took the assignment seriously. He possessed extraordinary organizational skills and ability. His zeal, dedication, and energy inspired every officer and private he led. He drilled, equipped, and led the Eighth Infantry to the front as readied fighting men in remarkable time. The regiment fought under the command of Generals Sherman, Burnside and Grant and was known as the "wandering regiment." After two years of service, Fenton's ailing health forced him to resign his commission.

Upon returning home to Flint, Colonel Fenton became the Democratic candidate for governor, but in the dominant Republican state, he had little chance of winning. He devoted himself to his profession and business, and he erected a block of downtown stores and a public hall in Flint. He was chosen as the chief engineer of the Flint Fire Department. In line with his nature, Fenton attacked the assignment with zeal and enthusiasm. Upon being alerted of a fire, in his haste, he ran into a post with such force that he sustained internal injuries. He died on November 12, 1871. His death was described in the local newspapers as follows:

This event cast a gloom over the entire city. Resolutions expressed over the great sorrow felt by the community were adopted at a public meeting of citizens. Similar resolutions were adopted by members of the bar, the common council of Flint, the fire department, and the Knights Templar Commandery, of which he was a member. On the day of his funeral, most of the businesses were closed and draped in mourning. He was a ripe scholar, an able lawyer, and a wise counselor. The elements of true manhood were combined in his character in such nearly perfect proportion that, as a man, neighbor, friend, and Christian gentleman, he won the entire confidence of his fellow citizens.

Fenton left behind four children. His beloved wife and companion of over thirty years had preceded him in death three years prior. Colonel William Matthew Fenton and his wife, Adelaide, both rest in peace within Glenwood Cemetery in Flint, Michigan.

CITY PARKS

The city of Fenton has nine parks that are located near the Shiawassee River and throughout the city. The parks bear the names of various residents whose service had a major effect on the community. The parks include Bush, Conklin, Franklin D. Adams, Freedom, Millpond, O'Donnell, Rackham, Silver Lake, and Strom. Two of the parks have historical significance: Millpond Park and Freedom Park.

MILLPOND PARK

Millpond Park, with its symbolic, iconic gazebo, sits nestled in a hollow next to the Shiawassee River. This access to fresh water was one of the main reasons Clark Dibble chose to purchase the forty-acre parcel.

When Clark Dibble first settled on his claimed parcel, he built a one-room log cabin on the edge of the water. A historic marker indicates its former location. Dibble used the water from the river to set up a sawmill that used an undershot wheel to generate power, taking advantage of the eight-foot drop in the river. The mill contained two blades. One upright saw blade was used to cut logs into planks; another, a circular saw, ripped the edges of the boards. Dibble had the sawmill running in the autumn of 1834, the same year he acquired his land. Clark sold his mill to his brother Wallace on July 12, 1837.

The Millpond Park gazebo. *Brenda Hasse.*

In 1840, William M. Fenton and Robert LeRoy built a flouring mill near the dam, which later burned.

Using the water from Millpond, the area around the waterway was transformed into an industrial park. Railroad tracks ran along the north side of the water and split into several branches for transporting and delivering products. Along the banks of the water was a storage bin for coal. The A.V.

Sunshine Fenton Mill. *Fenton Historical Society.*

Anderson barrel factory was located on Millpond across from the intersection of the South Pine and Ellen Streets intersection. Nestled between Millpond and Ellen Street was Cook Brothers Apple Evaporating Works and a cider mill and sawmill owned by D.T. Colwell. At one time, Walnut Street extended south of Ellen Street to Millpond. There was a flume that ran from Millpond to a lumber planer and sawmill owned by Colwell. Stacks of lumber surrounded the mill, waiting to be purchased and shipped. The water used from Millpond to operate the mill was returned to the Shiawassee River near the Leroy Street bridge.

In 1868, George Riker and Charles Adams built the Sunshine Fenton Mills along the natural drop in the river, replacing the mill built by Fenton and LeRoy. The building sat at approximately 301 South Leroy Street, the current location of Fenton City Hall. The partnership between the men dissolved, and a new partnership, Colwell and Adams, was announced in 1872. In May 1876, the Holly Dam collapsed, sending a wave of water toward Fenton, taking out the dam, the mills, and stacks of milled lumber. The boards and beams from the structures and lumber were swept down river, blocking the normal flow of the water at the railroad bridge east of Lincoln Street and causing a flood in the city. The mills that survived were kept idle until the dam could be repaired. Colwell bought out Adams in 1880. The mill changed hands before Colwell regained ownership. He sold it in 1900 to H.F. Bush. The mill continued to change hands over the years until it burned on June 3, 1921. The Fenton Light and Power Company, along with the Fenton Waterworks, also had buildings on the property.

Today, Millpond Park is a lovely community park that hosts summer concerts and weddings in the gazebo and often has children playing and fishing from its riverbanks.

FREEDOM PARK

Many of Fenton's past residents relocated from New York to make the settlement of Dibbleville and Fentonville their home. William Fenton donated the land that became the town square, which is now known as Freedom Park. Majestic houses still face the historic greenspace. Before leaving to fight in the Civil War, the men mustered at the town square. They bid their friends and families farewell, indicated they would send a letter when possible, and promised they would return.

The following is a list of the brave men of Fenton who were called to duty to fight in the Civil War:

Lewis C. Ackerman, George Adams, William E. Aldrich, John W. Banks, Charles F. Barber, George W. Barbour, Marcello Barnum, Edward N. Bennett, Andrew Bly, Benjamin Botsford, William Butcher, Moses Carr, George W. Case, Joseph Cathcart, Lemon B. Chappell, Amos K. Clark, Henry O. Clark, Thomas Clark, Joseph W. Cole, Laban Connor, Charles T. Conrad, Milo Crawford, Lewis V. Curry, Clark T. Dibble, Joel Dibble, Edward H. Dickerman, Wilson P. Donaldson, James A. Dunlap, Edgar Durfee, Palmer Eldridge, Edward F. Farnum, Charles Feckenscher, Asa H.

Left: Freedom Park marker. *Right*: Freedom Park Memorial. *Brenda Hasse.*

Fields, Alfred Ganson, John Ganson, James Giles, William H. Giles, Enos Golden, Theodore Grimson, Frank Hanmer, Albert E. Herrington, Edwin J. Hewitt, Edward S. Hirst, Thomas Holland, Andrew W. Holliday, George Hopkins, Dexter Horton, Edwin M. Hovey, Charles S. Johnson, Cash M. Jones, Carpenter Kimball, Jeremiah S. Knapp, Isaac H. Lawrence, Philander Linley, George Ludlow, Calvin L. Mann, Alvah H. Marsh, Benjamin F. Marsh, Asher E. Mather, F. Warren McComber, William Meginnes, Joseph W. Moore, Anson Morehouse, Edward A. Morey, Newton B. Morris, Marion Munson, Henry Osgood, John Owen, Daniel C. Parker, James W. Perry, Ebin Remington, David S. Rich, James W. Ripley, James S. Robinson, Amsey Rogers, Edwin Rogers, Chauncey P. Ryno, Thomas G. Skelton, Ezra St. John, Abner D. Swett, Clayton Taylor, Jonathan Terry, Seymour Thompson, John C. Thorpe, Charles Totten, Luke J. Tryon, Henry C. Van Atta, Daniel Varnum, Byron Vosburg, Elias B. Wightman, Ernest T. Winters, Charles F. Wortman, John M. Wright and Elbert A. Young.

Today, there are plans to update Freedom Park with a memorial to remember the men and women who have served in our military forces.

THE PARK CLUB

The residents living near Freedom Park formed a club. The first meeting of the Park Club was held at the home of Mr. and Mrs. Charles Damon in December 1916. The by-laws and regulations were discussed, passed, and signed by all members. Qualifications for membership were as follows: (1) the member must be a parent of one or more children, and (2) each individual must be able and willing to sing, dance, play, tell a good story, pass sandwiches, or do some stunt to make the meetings more enjoyable. Bimonthly meetings were hosted by families, rotating to the next house to the right around the park. Meetings would begin at 7:00 p.m. and end at 10:00 p.m. Guests understood that they were to leave promptly without being asked. Food was budgeted to cost five cents or less per plate. With the business of the evening out of the way, Daman entertained guests with his adventurous stories until the smoke in the room became thick. Then the men adjourned to his gun room, where the stories continued.

RAILROAD TRANSPORTATION

The Detroit, Grand Haven and Milwaukee Railroad came to Fentonville in 1856. It carried passengers who were eager to settle within the village, visitors, traveling salesmen known as "drummers," posted mail and other cargo. The train would stop near the wooden depot located on the north side of the tracks east of the grain elevator. Passengers disembarked and were either transported to their destinations via horse and buggy or walked a short distance to the hotel for some needed rest or a meal after their trip. Various cargo was unloaded from the train and either delivered or picked up. In April 1870, Miss Susan B. Anthony arrived and lectured to a good-sized audience in the Colwell Hall on the subject of "Work, Wages, and the Ballot." It was reported in the *Fenton Independent* that she spoke in a calm and earnest manner, conveying her sincerity in her desire for women to obtain the right to vote and the disparity of education and wages. She claimed the only remedy for women was to gain the right to vote.

In 1882, the present-day depot made of red and yellow brick was built on the south side of the railroad tracks. Mr. Eddy's coaches awaited each train's arrival to transport passengers to hotels and other destinations. Cargo continued to be unloaded at the old wooden depot, and goods were either delivered or picked up by recipients. The village seemed to come alive with excitement when a circus arrived via the rail system. Barefoot children watched in anticipation as the tent was erected in the depot yard. In 1883, P.T. Barnum's circus arrived, and its main feature was Jumbo the

Fentonville depots and train. *Fenton Historical Society.*

Fentonville depot. *Fenton Historical Society.*

elephant. The Fred H. Wren Company performed *Uncle Tom's Cabin* to large audiences. For ten or fifteen cents, a patron could enter the tent and watch the nightly performance.

Also arriving by train were men with monkeys dressed in velvet suits. They played their crank organs while touring the streets of the village. The monkey would tip its hat when a penny was placed in its tin cup. In 1879, a dancing bear performed on Leroy Street. The Colwell Opera House hosted *General Tom Thumb and Company*. Because of the show's popularity, it was performed on several occasions.

Other notables who arrived by train and visited Fenton were Schuyler Colfax, President Ulysses S. Grant's vice president during his first term; Lillian Langtry; Mrs. Jarley's wax figures in 1903; *Pawnee Bill's Wild West Show* in 1905; the Boston Boomer Girls baseball team that played the Fenton Nine in 1902; and the highly acclaimed *Florida on Wheels*, which gave patrons, for the cost of ten cents, a glimpse at chained alligators and other creatures. The train also traveled from Fenton to Detroit for patrons to watch and listen to Adelina Patti, a great singing diva who performed her farewell concert tour in the city.

The brick depot caught fire in 1923 and was rebuilt. In 1960, Grand Trunk Railroad closed the station and no longer allowed passenger trains.

Ladies of the Night

When it came to female entertainment, Fentonville offered several places for lonely gentlemen to visit. The least expensive rooms on the upper floors of the various hotels were sometimes rented out to prostitutes. There was also a house on Second Street that offered such entertainment for men. Rumors that continue to this day indicate the second floor above 105 West Shiawassee Avenue in the Andrews Block and the house at the southwest corner of Elizabeth and Adelaide Streets were also brothels. Recently, a gentleman with a metal detector found several pieces of costume jewelry on an empty lot behind the former Riggs Hotel, which was in the vicinity of the A.J. Phillips Fenton Museum. The items are on display in the museum along with a key to one of the hotel rooms.

Railroad Workers

When a train stopped at the Fentonville depot with a scheduled layover before it had to depart for its next destination, the workers on the train sometimes took the opportunity to visit their favorite lady who offered her companionship for an hour or so. The train's conductor would order the men who requested a leave to take a lantern with them before departing from the depot yard. The glass globes of these railroad lanterns were red in color. The men were instructed to put the lanterns outside the buildings

Flint and Holly Railroad. The H.H. Carpo train. *Fenton Historical Society*.

they were in or in a widow so they could be easily located. If their train's departure time was drawing near and the workers had not returned, the conductor would know exactly where to find them. Some say this is how the nickname "red-light district" came about. It was also possible that over time, the women offering their services would display similar lanterns, indicating they were available.

An Embarrassing Moment

One particularly lonely night—or perhaps after a fight with his misses—a gentleman, whom we shall refrain from naming, decided to call on a prostitute for an hour or two. During his visit, he hung his pants on the bedpost. When he went to put them back on, he discovered the money that was in his pocket had been stolen. In his rage, he notified the authorities and filed a report of the theft. However, since all crimes are posted in the local newspapers, those who read it became aware of how and where he had spent his evening.

Residential Haunts

Some may not think much of things that go bump in the night, but for those who reside in historic houses within Fenton, they think twice when strange things happen and the unexplainable occurs. Below are a few of the reported residential hauntings in and around the city.

High Street

This glorious old home serenades its residents while they sleep. Chamber and classical music can occasionally be heard here, waking the homeowners in the middle of the night. When they rise to investigate, they discover their radio and television are both turned off. The owners researched the history of their home and discovered that two maiden ladies once lived and taught piano lessons in the house. The homeowners tracked the music and discovered it was coming from the attic, and it occurred shortly after they began remodeling the house. The gifted spirits may have disagreed with the owners' choice of wallpaper and paint color. One day, the owners' brother went into the home's basement. When he rejoined his sister upstairs, he stated there was a ghost in the house, because one had brushed by him while he was downstairs.

Another homeowner on the same street experienced a heavy bag of groceries being knocked to the floor and heard her name being called by a disembodied voice. However, she was the only one in the house at the time.

This house, built around 1860, is inhabited by the spirit of an elderly woman who wears an apron over her dress. She likes to peek over the shoulder of the gentleman who resides in the house, and she watches him while he works on projects, such as repairing the pipes beneath the kitchen sink. The gentleman also once heard his name called by a female voice when he was alone in the house. He has also seen dark shadow figures in his peripheral vision.

South Holly Road

This elegant Victorian house was built in 1870. It has changed hands and undergone several additional construction projects over the years. Its present owner claims to have witnessed the apparition of a funeral in the parlor. The woman saw a man standing at attention near a casket, as if guarding it. What she witnessed was a military vigil. The deceased and past homeowner had fought in several battles of the Civil War. The resident watched as

Cement casket inscribed "BABY." *Brenda Hasse*.

several people came to visit the body through the north porch door and exited through a wall. At one time, a door existed where the apparitions were exiting. During one of the home's renovations, a business journal and rosary were discovered inside a wall. Two small cement caskets were unearthed when the garage was added to the house. One had "BABY" written in stone on the cement lid. Apparently, when the Michigan basement was updated with a cement floor, the bones of the babies were discovered in the dirt. It is assumed the cement caskets were made for the deceased infants' remains at that time.

The homeowners often hear thuds and footsteps echoing from the second floor and the scraping of kitchen stools sliding across the floor when sitting in an adjoining room. While one of their children was studying in a second-floor room, a white mist floated by him.

Rockwell Street

This historic home was once owned by a loving bee-keeping couple. The wife would grow beautiful flowers to keep her winged, buzzing friends happy. The bees were known to make the sweetest honey in town. The couple would harvest the honey and hand out small jars to trick-or-treating children at Halloween. During the winter months, the couple allowed the local piano teacher, who lived up a steep hill, to instruct her students using the piano in their living room. The accommodation made it easier for the children to walk to their lessons, rather than struggling up the icy incline with their leather-soled shoes. During one piano lesson, the student had caught a cold and continued to cough throughout the time with his teacher. Assuming the child had a scratchy, sore throat, the homeowner heated a bit of honey for the student to soothe his cough. Once word got around to the other children of the couple's delicious remedy, the piano teacher's enrollment for lessons increased. The present owner has reported the upstairs shower turning on by itself and books on a living room shelf being pushed deep into the bookcase until they touch the back. A young visitor claimed to see the apparition of a man in blue bib overalls and referred to him as "the blue man." The homeowner's dog often stands at the top of the basement stairs and freezes, refusing to descend the steps.

Another resident on Rockwell Street claims to have seen the apparition of an empty pair of men's work pants suspended in midair in her dining room as she exited her kitchen. She paused, and as she stared at the pants' back pockets, she watched the apparition disappear. Taken aback, she blinked her eyes several times, questioning if what she had seen was real. While watching television with her husband, who sat in a separate chair, her ponytail was pulled and flipped upward into the air. The resident male spirit appears to be watchful and protective of the house and those within it. The couple forgot to extinguish a candle one night before going to bed. When they woke the following day, it had been snuffed out instead of being allowed to continue to burn in the glass container.

Main Street

This disgruntled spirit often lets its presence be known. For example, the residents had trouble keeping the center candle in an antique floor-style candelabra in place. The unlit candle would often flip out of the holder and fly across the room. Even when the owner drips candle wax in the holder before inserting the taper to secure it, the spirit persistently succeeds in ejecting the candle. The homeowners have also heard a growling sound on the second floor.

The residents of another house on this street reached out to a psychic medium for answers to the strange happenings they were experiencing. During the medium's visit, everyone heard the disembodied cry of a child and the sound of footsteps.

This household also hosted a psychic phenomenon class. People entered the house in pairs and meditated. They reported seeing an old lady and experienced an unexplainable force that pushed them down the stairs.

South Adelaide Street

The family of this household reported seeing a misty face in a mirror—a past resident, perhaps.

In another home, the resident often experiences their heavy front door flying open, hears weighted footsteps and feels as if someone was trying to push them down the stairway.

North Adelaide Street

The resident in this house has a spirit that makes itself at home. When the homeowner wakes in the morning, she often inhales the aroma of freshly brewed coffee. However, when she enters the kitchen, coffee has not been made.

Shiawassee Avenue

This spiritually active home woke its residents at 2:00 a.m. with the dining room door slamming shut. On a separate occasion, a guest woke one night, and at the foot of her bed stood the apparition of a woman dressed in an older-style gown with her hair styled atop her head. The female guest recalled the strong fragrance of perfume within the room and swears she would easily be able to recognize it again.

Elizabeth Street

The residents who live in the grand houses along Elizabeth Street across from Freedom Park, once the town square, have experienced unexplainable occurrences, such as doors opening by themselves and the sounds of echoing footsteps and disembodied voices. One concerned mother whose daughter lived in one of the houses feared for her daughter's life. She was relieved when her daughter moved out of the house.

Another homeowner kept hearing a disembodied voice. She thought it was her deceased husband conveying his displeasure in his wife's decision to throw his sister out of the house.

Park Street

The spirit in this house likes to keep the owners guessing. They will set something down, such as their car keys, only to find they have been moved to a different location when they go to retrieve them later.

SOUTH LEROY STREET

The lady of this house has experienced a foul odor whenever her husband is out of town or working late. The pungent smell has been detected by the couple's children as well.

THE FENTON HOTEL TAVERN AND GRILLE

This historic building has stood the test of time on the corner of North Leroy and Main Streets. The Fenton Hotel Tavern and Grille is known as one of the most haunted bars and restaurants in the United States. Its reputation of serving delicious meals continues as it did when the tavern was first built by Mr. Seed and Mr. Flint in 1856, the year the railroad came to Fentonville. It was called the Vermont House then, and Mr. Seed was the manager. The *Fenton Independent* listed Abner Roberts as the proprietor of the town's largest hotel in 1868, the Fenton House at that time.

In 1872, the Mystic Seven, a secret social organization with a symbol of a 7 intersecting a crescent moon comprising the original seven young men of Fenton, held its third anniversary banquet at the hotel. Since the society's organization in 1869, it had grown substantially to include some thirty members. They enjoyed a mouthwatering feast that included over three dozen dishes of meat, sauces, vegetables, and desserts. Many of the group's original members were in attendance, including C.A. Gower, Mort H. Stanford, Ellery Anderson, James H. Waterman, Charles W. Cornwall, John J. Cornwall, and Tom H. Davis. The purpose of the organization was to support cultural and social advancement. The group enjoyed a total of four annual meetings before its members moved away from Fenton to begin other endeavors. They held another Mystic Seven reunion in 1901; they took the trolley to Long Lake and enjoyed a picnic on the banks, toured the lake in the majestic boat *City of Fenton* and returned to the Colwell Opera House for a reception and banquet.

DeNio Hotel. *Fenton Historical Society.*

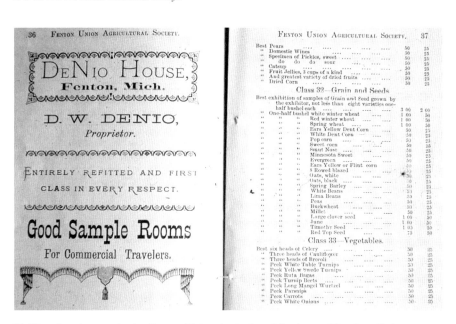

DeNio advertisement in the Fenton Union Agricultural Society publication. *Fenton Historical Society.*

After the tavern changed ownership and management over the years, D.W. DeNio purchased it and renamed it the DeNio House in 1882. He thoroughly overhauled the interior of the building with a fresh coat of paint and wallpapering, and he refurnished it in style. The following year, he repainted the exterior of the hotel, sodded a ten-foot section in front, and planted trees. The DeNio House was the first building in Fenton to subscribe to a telephone in 1883. In 1886, a billiard room, bar, and sample room were added. A hall that was thirty by eighty feet was used for public parties. For the grand opening party, Mrs. DeNio prepared a splendid meal for two hundred members of the distinguished Carpediem Club. An orchestra from Owosso provided music for dancing. The DeNio House earned the reputation of being the best-kept house between Detroit and Grand Rapids. The hotel's barn could house and care for one hundred horses. DeNio sold the hotel in 1887 to Major L.L. Andress. The new owner renamed it Fenton House, and he expanded its picturesque porches to run the entire length of the second and third floors.

Mr. Hurd became the hotel's proprietor in 1898. He built a new brick kitchen that was twenty by thirty feet, installed a steam heating plant and fixed up the employee rooms on the second floor. On February 17, 1904, John Moyer's team of horses ran away from the depot, darted across a sidewalk, and straddled the supporting posts of the hotel's porches. The horses pulled the posts from their cement bases, causing the porches to collapse. The team of horses managed to stay ahead of the wreckage, remaining unharmed, and were stopped once they crossed Leroy Street and entered Potter's wood yard. Even though many of the hotel's windows were broken during the unfortunate accident, no one was injured. Men quickly cleaned up the damage without interrupting the flow of business. In the spring, only the second-floor porch was rebuilt. T.J. Dumanois became the hotel's proprietor in 1916. Prohibition caused a downturn in business, and the hotel closed for a time. In 1933, when Prohibition was repealed, the hotel reopened. Over time, the hotel was used less as a hotel and more as a restaurant and banquet hall. Mr. and Mrs. Ray and Ann O'Reilly owned the Hotel Fenton in 1946.

As it was back then, the Fenton Hotel is still renowned for its delicious food. But those who have dined at this establishment may also be aware of and have experienced its hauntings.

As today's visitors enter the historic building, just off the tin-ceilinged foyer sits the most active area in the hotel—the bar. Staff members often hear their names called by disembodied voices and are sometimes tapped on their heads or touched elsewhere on their bodies, only to find no one else is there. Some have also witnessed wine glasses jumping off the rack, flying across the room and shattering on the floor. One guest informed a female bartender that he watched someone hug her, yet she could not see or feel anyone nearby. Table 32 is often visited by a man who orders a Jack Daniels on the rocks. But when the drink is served, the man is nowhere to be found. Sometimes, this man includes his order with that of whoever is sitting at "his" table. Could his desire for his favorite drink continue in the afterlife?

Even though the upper two floors of the building are now used for only storage, at one time, former guests stayed in the small rooms for the night. A permanent resident, Emery, lived in a corner room and was the hotel's elderly custodian. Dining guests can often hear his pacing footsteps in his room above while they enjoy their meal.

When the rooms were let out, the least expensive rooms were located on the third floor. Prostitutes may have rented a room or two on this floor. One of these said "ladies of the night" discovered she was with child and hanged herself in the third stall of the ladies' bathroom. Women often report seeing her apparition within the third stall and have felt a cold spot within the room. Another indicated her hair was pulled while using the stall.

Other patrons report seeing a black cat that disappears, an apparition of a tall man in a top hat, and lights that seem to shut off by themselves. Some have also heard someone's voice making an announcement on the bar speakers, even though they are turned off. Employees who visit the upper floors report hearing a disembodied female voice that seems to whisper to them on the third floor, and they have seen a bearded man's apparition outside a second-story window. Perhaps the well-dressed gentleman is standing on the balcony that is no longer there.

Patrons who dine at the Fenton Hotel agree that some of its guests from the past never checked out.

THE HORTON FAMILY

One of the most iconic families to live in Fenton was the Dexter Horton family. The Horton family tree can be traced back to 1640, when Joseph Lee and Hannah Horton boarded the ship *Shadow* in Leichester, England. They landed in Hampton, Massachusetts, where Joseph build hist first house on the eastern part of Long Island.

DEXTER HORTON

On June 24, 1836, Dexter Horton was born in Groveland, Oakland County, Michigan, in a log cabin built by his father, Henry Wisner Horton, on 360 acres of land. At age fourteen, Dexter attended Albion College. He was known as a good student, excelling in his studies, and was well liked by his teachers and classmates. However, his studies were cut short when he was expelled for mischievous behavior. At that time, he was president of the Eclectic Society. Upon his return home, he taught school in the winter and farmed in the summer until he became of age. He left home with two colts and fifteen bags of corn and took up residence in Fenton. He began selling agricultural implements and was known, in the twenty years of his business's operation, as one of the largest retail dealers in this part of the state. During the 1860 presidential campaign, Dexter took an active role in promoting the election of Abraham Lincoln. As a young man, Dexter was active in politics, voting for the Whig Party and later becoming a Republican. He held the office of postmaster of Fenton. On April 25, 1861, Dexter married Lavina Losee, and they were blessed with five children: Glenn L., who passed away at five months old; Mary Ann; Mabel Fasquella; Bryson Dexter; and Elmira H., or Myra, as she liked to be called.

When the Civil War began, Dexter, supporting President Lincoln, worked diligently to hold meetings and recruit men throughout the region. In 1863, he joined the Light Horse Artillery of the Army of the Potomac. President Lincoln appointed Dexter as the captain and commissary of subsistence in 1864. Horton joined the armies in Tennessee and Georgia until the close of the war. He was a participant in the Atlanta campaign and marched with Sherman to the sea. He also took part in the Carolinas campaigns. He was promoted to the rank of major. When he returned home, Major Horton was reappointed postmaster but was removed from the position for political reasons. He was a delegate to the Soldier's Convention, held in Chicago, that nominated General Grant for the presidency.

Major Dexter Horton was appointed assistant sergeant-at-arms of the state senate in 1867. Two years later, he became a representative in the state legislature. Major Horton, along with David Colwell, built the Colwell Opera House, located on the southeast corner of Leroy and Caroline Streets. The building was used from 1869 to 1975 and housed an opera house on the second floor, which was used by churches, schools, and fraternal organizations. A U.S. post office was located on the first floor. The brickwork on the front of the building was marked with "FLT," which is a symbol for the Independent Order of the Odd Fellows fraternal organization. The building's last use was as a dime store. It has since been moved to Crossroads Village in Flint, Michigan.

Major Horton was commander of Fenton Post, no. 24., of the Grand Army of the Republic for seven years. He was also a Mason for thirty years, one of the trustees of the First Presbyterian Church and the president of the school board for twelve years. Major Horton served on the village council and was president of the village. He also served as the president of the Fenton Agricultural Society, the Electric Light and Power Association, and the Genesee Pioneers Picnic Association, and he served as chief of the Fenton Hook and Ladder Company (Fenton Fire Department).

The Horton family lived at 118 West Shiawassee Avenue. Major Dexter Horton died on December 28, 1901, and was buried in section C of Oakwood Cemetery.

MARY ANN HORTON RACKHAM

Mary Ann Horton was born on September 1, 1864. She married Horace Hatcher Rackham. Horace was a lawyer and philanthropist who made his money by investing in Henry Ford's auto business. The couple were members and generous contributors of the First Presbyterian Church. They also were instrumental in funding the Fenton Community Center, Christian Science building, and the Fenton Fire Hall and Jail. The City of Detroit and the University of Michigan received funds from their trust. The couple, along with their infant children, were entombed in a marble and brass mausoleum at the Evergreen Cemetery in Detroit.

BRYSON DEXTER HORTON

Bryson Dexter Horton graduated from Fenton High School in 1890. He attended the University of Michigan. His roommate was a fellow Fenton High School classmate, Mark S. Knapp, who became a medical doctor. Bryson graduated with a bachelor of science degree in engineering in 1895 and earned a varsity letter in track while there.

After earning his degree, Bryson became the assistant engineer for the Detroit Park and Boulevard Commission in 1897. A year later, he became the outside superintendent. He is credited with wiring many of the houses in Fenton with electricity.

When the war between the United States and Spain began in 1898, Bryson enlisted in the U.S. Navy. He was commissioned as the chief electrician on the USS *Yosemite*. After the war, he returned to Detroit and was promoted to the position of chief engineer for the Detroit Public Lighting Commission. In 1900, Bryson went to Morenci, Arizona, and was an electrical engineer for Phelps, Dodge and Company at its copper smelting plants.

Shortly after his father's death on December 28, 1901, Bryson and his partner James B. McCarthy started the McBride Manufacturing Company. He also organized the Detroit Fuse and Manufacturing Company as its president.

After reading stories regarding the lighting of Menlo Park in New Jersey, he recalled an invention he created years before: the arcless electric fuse. He founded the Square D Manufacturing Company in Detroit and began production of the fuse. He was the president of the

Bryson Dexter Horton. *Fenton Historical Society*.

company until his retirement in 1928. The company changed its name to Square D in 1917 and later became Schneider Electric. The company built its first power distribution panelboard in 1926. Three years later, it moved into industrial control after merging with Industrial Controller Company, based in Milwaukee, and began producing circuit breakers under a license from Westinghouse.

After his retirement, Bryson became the chairman of the Horace H. and Mary A. Rackham Trust Fund in 1934. Mary Rackham, his sister, was the wife of Horace H. Rackham, an attorney. The University of Michigan received $9.7 million from the trust in the form of a grant. The trust provided funding for the construction and maintenance of the Fenton Community Center, the Fenton Fire Hall and Jail facility, and the Christian Science Church of Fenton. The trust also donated to the Horace H. Rackham Educational building in Detroit and the Rackham Schools of Special Education in Michigan and Florida. It also provided funding for the fountain and reflection pool at the entrance of the Detroit Zoological Park.

In 1939, Bryson Dexter Horton received an honorary doctoral degree in engineering from the University of Michigan for his inventions and contributions to education and philanthropy.

The original and still operational 1922 Square D model, which encompassed an electrical safety switch that helped American factory workers work in a safer environment, was donated to the Smithsonian National Museum of American History in Washington, D.C., by Schneider Electric of Palatine, Illinois, in November 2003. The donation was made on the one hundredth anniversary of the Square D brand.

Bryson died on December 14, 1945, at the University of Michigan Hospital in Ann Arbor. He was buried in section C of Oakwood Cemetery. Part of his estate, 544 acres bordering Fagan Lake in Holly, Michigan, was donated and became the Great Lakes National Cemetery. Its first burial occurred in October 2005. Bryson was inducted posthumously into the Fenton High School Hall of Fame in 2009. Bryson was truly a pioneer in his field of study who continues to influence lives today.

Elmira "Myra" H. Horton Bussey

The youngest of the Horton children was Elmira H. Horton. Many knew her by her nickname, "Myra." Elmira was born on June 12, 1873. She married Charles Luther Bussey, a local business retailer, on February 6, 1901. Along with her sister, Mary, Elmira was an active member of the First Presbyterian Church, was instrumental in overseeing its restoration and maintenance, and organized the purchase of a new organ.

THE FENTON FIRE HALL

The lack of volunteers was never an issue when a fire was raging somewhere in Fentonville—it was the lack of necessary equipment needed to put them out that was the most dangerous threat to any building or even the entire town. After several devastating fires, on March 9, 1875, the Fenton Hook and Ladder Company No. 1 was established. Over the next four years, Fentonville acquired much-needed firefighting equipment, including a pump, hook and ladder, hoses, wagons, rubber pails, et cetera. The Fenton Fire Hall was built in 1879 to store its firefighting equipment. The building was an elegant two-story structure located north of the Shiawassee River on the west side of Leroy Street at approximately 105 South Leroy Street. It also housed the city hall on the second floor that was used for meetings and other gatherings. In 1883, cisterns used to collect rainwater were installed in several locations throughout the city. Hoses were attached to a hydrant, and the pump would pull the water from the cistern when fighting fires.

The original fire hall was demolished shortly after the Fenton Community Center was built in 1937. The Horace H. and Mary A. Rackham Trust Fund provided the funds needed for the new fire hall and jail that was located at 201 South Leroy Street in 1938. In 2002, the Fenton Fire Department moved to its new location at 205 East Caroline Street, leaving the location on South Leroy Street vacant.

The Michigan Brewing Company renovated the vacant Fenton Fire Hall. Keeping the theme of the city's volunteer firefighters in mind, the

The Hook and Ladder Fire Department. *Fenton Historical Society.*

Woodworth Plumbing, Fenton Fire Hall, and Wolcott Milling Company on South Leroy Street in 1937 before construction of the Fenton Community Center. *Fenton Historical Society.*

The Fenton Fire Hall. *Brenda Hasse.*

company opened the Fenton Fire Hall Restaurant in December 2013. A resident ghost that the staff has affectionately named Hank currently haunts the location. Hank likes to break coffee pots, knock things over and turn the lights off and on. He has been known to switch the bathroom lights off while it is in use, leaving the occupant in the dark. The staff believes Hank is harmless, but this mischievous spirit likes to make his presence known.

One staff member described a day when she was a bit shaken. She swore Hank passed through her. She was talking to a coworker when, suddenly, she could not hear anything, even though she was yelling. She said she thought she was talking at a normal volume. Next, she felt a pit in her stomach, her feet went numb, and the air was knocked out of her.

Could Hank have been a fallen volunteer fireman, or a person housed in the jail? Maybe he feels comfortable in the familiar surroundings and decided to stay.

FENTON WATERWORKS

As the population of Fenton continued to increase into 1884, its citizens still obtained their drinking water from wells on their properties. Most had cisterns and water barrels to collect rainwater. Since many households had chickens, goats, other animals, and outhouses in the back corners of their yards, oftentimes, wells would "go bad" from contamination. Once a well was contaminated, that household was forced to borrow well water from a neighbor. It was common for Fenton's residents to suffer from typhoid fever and dysentery.

Ease of accessing water was also important in putting out fires, which could spread quickly in the village. Sometimes, the best defense against the consuming flames was to tear down adjacent buildings.

In 1886, Dexter Horton, the village president, pointed out that a change in the charter must first occur to get a waterworks system in place. He stated, "The principal argument in favor of waterworks is the protection from fire. As it now is, nine-tenths of the residence portion of our village is absolutely without protection. The fire engine is an excellent protection for the main street and adjacent localities but could not reach the outskirts of the village

The Fenton Waterworks. *Brenda Hasse.*

in time to save anything but property adjoining the fire." Delays in obtaining funding put the project off.

In the autumn of 1888, an epidemic of illness swept through Fenton. A letter written to the editor of the *Fenton Independent* was printed on the front page: "The majority of the sickness and deaths from malaria and typhoid fever occurring in Fenton this past fall might be attributed to the imbibing of impure drinking water. There is scarcely a family in Fenton that has escaped the poisonous effects of their well water, but I have examined the water from three different wells in different parts of the town and not one but would have been condemned immediately by the most tyro-sanitary committee.—JDR." The letter was written by John D. Riker, a medical student at the University of Michigan. By June 1889, progress on the project had yet to begin.

In August 1889, the Coe Manufacturing Drill Works Company, located on the southeast corner of East Shiawassee Avenue and Oak Street, caught fire. The firemen responded to the alarm and arrived at the scene promptly. However, the water level in Millpond was so low that the engine could not pump water and had to be relocated to another area where the bank was lower. This cost valuable time. Coe's Drill Works and Mac Walker's Fenton Iron Works, located south of Coe's building, were able to use their steam pumps to keep the fire from spreading to nearby buildings. After the heavy loss of the building, fittings, and patterns for various drills, plans were developed for the Fenton Waterworks. On September 12, 1889, citizens were allowed to voice their opinions by voting. Those who had lost their jobs at Coe's Drill Works were joined by Mac Walker's Fenton Iron Works workers and went to the polls as a reckoning force to cast their vote. The measure easily passed, with a vote of 459 to 53. Two weeks later, the Holdrige Evaporating Works (Cook's Brothers Evaporating Works) was destroyed by fire. The contract for a waterworks system was quickly awarded to Mac Walker. The installation of a waterworks system, which included the foundation of a pumping house that was laid near the corner of South Leroy and Ellen Streets, trenches for the pipe, and hydrants began immediately. Progress was reported weekly in the *Fenton Independent*. The only accident recorded occurred when Pat Murphy was in a trench laying pipe in the block of the Colwell Opera House, at approximately 111 South Leroy Street, and there was a cave-in. The sand and gravel buried him up to his neck. Since Pat was sixty years old, it was assumed he suffered injuries to his aging body that were more serious than they initially believed and caused his death. Perhaps he was taken back to the waterworks building, where he died. Could his lingering and unrestful spirit be the prankster ghost at the Fenton Fire Hall Restaurant?

THE ANDREWS BUILDING

The Andrews Building is located on the south corner of the three-way stop at West Shiawassee Avenue and Leroy Street. This two-story brick structure was built in 1867 by C. Andrews. It has four storefronts, numbered accordingly. The second story, now apartments, was once an office for the Ladies' Library Association and the *Fenton Independent*. It is also rumored that a brothel operated on the second floor above no. 3, which is now 105 West Shiawassee Avenue.

The first tenant in no. 1 was Booth and Boutell. The merchants sold books, jewelry, and music. In 1885, John W. Davis claimed the storefront, sold groceries, and was a druggist. He was followed by Charles L. Carrigan, who sold boots and shoes, in 1886. In no. 2, P.M. Anderson sold hats and men's clothing. A. Curtiss took over the storefront in 1872 and sold clothes, followed by Burdick Potter, who sold feeds, in 1883. The first business in no. 3 was Mr. and Mrs. Johnson and Company. It was a crockery store that sold fine china, everyday dishware, tea sets, glassware, and silverware. Mrs. Johnson was a millinery and made lovely hats. In 1887, I. G. Buell Sewing Machines occupied the space. Justice Elihu Waite moved into the storefront in 1900 and opened a hardware store the following year.

Elihu Waite was born on June 16, 1830. When he was twenty-six years old, he moved from New York to Fentonville with his wife and seven children. His first wife, Elizabeth, passed away in 1887. He became Fenton's justice of the peace in 1893. In 1900, he moved his office from East Shiawassee Avenue to no. 3 Andrews Building. He retired as Fenton's justice of the peace, married Myra Elizabeth Tomkinson and opened a hardware store in the same location in 1901. In his later years, Elihu became senile and died at the age of eighty-five from the grippe (the flu). Myra joined him in eternal peace seven days later.

In 1929, Mrs. Julia Tryon operated an upholstery shop from Elihu's former hardware store location. In 1943, Doctor John Book, a chiropractor, administered to his patients there. The storefront became the home of a bookstore in 2010. In 2011, Fenton's Open Book Bookstore opened its doors for business, and today, it hosts many events, such as author signings and community events. It offers its customers a selection of various books, toys, and gifts.

In no. 4, J.M. Adams operated a hardware, tin, and stoves business. E.N. Chandler sold hardware and Detroit stoves from the same location in 1872, followed by A.K. Clark, a grocer, in 1887. Around the corner of the building on Leroy Street was Judge Daniel LeRoy's office. He was Robert LeRoy's father. Judge LeRoy was the last attorney general for the Michigan Territory and the first attorney general for the State of Michigan. He also practiced law in Fenton.

Paranormal activity has been reported in some of the current businesses that now occupy the historic Andrews Building. However, Fenton's Open Book has a particularly vibrant spirit. Book lovers from near and far who visit the bookstore have experienced books flying from the shelves, smelled the fragrance of cigar or pipe smoke lingering in the air, felt a tug on their clothing, and heard strange noises, such as a cart rolling across the floor and footsteps.

A medium who visited the bookstore indicated there is a portal on the east wall that has spirits coming and going.

One bookstore customer was drawn to a small basket that contained necklace pendants made of glass. She could hear the glass clinking as if the jewelry was being sorted through or shifted. As she stared into the basket, nothing was moving, yet she continued to hear the glass being moved in the container.

An employee arrived to open the bookstore one morning when she kept hearing strange noises. Hoping to calm the spirit, the employee greeted Elihu, announced she was going to take a few pictures with her cellphone and asked if he would like to be in one of them. She took a photograph of a bookshelf near the front counter and snapped a second picture. Much to her surprise, the second photograph had a strange glowing blur in it. She kindly thanked Elihu before unlocking the front door for customers.

During an author book signing in December 2012, the bookstore hosted four authors. The authors sat at their assigned tables behind their displayed books. When there was a lull in customer traffic, they chatted among themselves. With no one near the authors' books at the time, all four of one of the author's displayed books were simultaneously knocked off the wire bookstands and slammed down onto the table. The authors stopped talking and looked at the books. One commented, "That was weird." Aware of the store's haunting, the author returned her books to the bookstands and reassured everyone that the bookstore ghost was to blame—he was just making his presence known. Several hours later, the same author had her books knocked down a second time.

One Saturday afternoon, a local resident was walking up and down the aisles, looking at books on the shelves, when he was startled by a loud bang behind him. He turned to see a large coffee table book on the floor. Turning to an employee, he stated, "I didn't touch that book." She grinned and replied, "I know. The bookstore ghost is responsible for knocking it off the shelf. It happens all the time. Eli must know that you have the ability to see or communicate with spirits. He was just trying to get your attention." The customer picked up the book and returned it to the shelf. Since it was such a large and heavy hardcover book, he assumed it may have tipped and fallen from the shelf. He tried to tilt the book downward, simulating how it may have fallen. However, the book was so large that the hardcover hit the shelf above and would not fall. The book had to be pulled from the shelf before it could fall to the floor.

Several other visitors have also experienced books falling from the shelves. Unaware of the bookstore ghost, they simply pick up the book and return it to the shelf. Some of the customers purchase the book they retrieve from the floor. Perhaps the ghost knows what each customer likes to read.

Visitors with psychic abilities indicate that Elihu hovers in the left top corner of the west display window. He must like the bird's-eye view.

The store's owner has experienced objects, which have remained in place for several years, being shifted, moved, or dropped on the floor. On one occasion, a customer inquired about a poster on foam board that was displayed on the top of the bookcase. The owner informed her that the poster has been there for years. Later that evening, when she reopened the bookstore for an evening event, the poster had been moved and was nearly falling from the bookcase. The owner opens the bookstore each morning and often discovers various items strewn about the floor that were put there during closing hours.

The owner once opened the bookstore to find an autumn decoration that had been hung from a string of lights on the floor. The leaf made of felt had been secured with a paperclip, making it nearly impossible for it to have fallen from where it was hung. While the owner was sitting beneath the very same string of lit lights, they flashed off and then turned back on. It was strange that the other independently powered lights did not flash off and on at the same time.

After operating the bookstore for over a decade, the owner received confirmation about which ghostly spirit was haunting it. One day, a group of women entered the bookstore. They were waiting for their reservation at a restaurant located at the end of the block. One of the women approached the counter and asked the owner if the bookstore was haunted. The owner indicated it was, and she assumed it may be haunted by the spirit of Elihu Waite. The customer, who was also a medium, began to get a headache, which indicated a spirit was near. She confirmed the spirit within the bookstore had become senile in their past life. Since the bookstore owner had researched the former tenants, she knew right away her friendly ghost was indeed Elihu Waite. Could Elihu believe he still owns a hardware store within the walls of no. 3 of the Andrews Building? If you care to visit his grave, it is located in section E of Oakwood Cemetery. His grave marker is engraved with the years of his birth and death. No other inscription dons the marker. When you visit Fenton's Open Book, don't be surprised if a book falls to the floor. Eli is offering his assistance, and you just may like the book he has selected for you to read.

THE HENRY RIGGS RESIDENCE

At age ten, Henry Clay Riggs was one of the first settlers to arrive from Grumlaw with his parents. He became an attorney and druggist.

Riggs purchased property from William Fenton and built his house at 207 West Shiawassee Avenue in 1856. This Federal-style house, square in shape, is listed in the National Register of Historic Places. At one time, a large porch extended the length of the back of the house. There was also a trapdoor in the loft that led to the carriage house below. This house was used as a stop on the Underground Railroad to hide escaped enslaved people. Beneath the dining room is a secret room. It may also be accessed through the carriage house. Henry and his wife, Martha, lived in the house for many years.

In 1870, Henry wrote and published *Historical Incidents*, which lists the names of the area's early settlers and describes how men camped by the Dibbles' mill at night while erecting a log cabin for their families during the day. He also confirmed the Dustin Cheney cabin was the first to be built in Dibbleville.

The various owners of this house have claimed to have been visited by many ghosts. As a result, the home has earned the reputation of being the most haunted house in Fenton.

One such haunting occurred on a summer evening while the woman's husband was away. She woke from sleeping and saw an apparition of a woman dressed in an old-fashioned long gown standing at the foot of her bed. As the spirit turned away, the homeowner noticed the spirit's long, flowing hair cascading down her back. The resident watched as the ghostly

The residence of Henry Clay and Martha Riggs. *Fenton Historical Society.*

figure seemed to search for something in the room. A year later, a gentleman apparition dressed in the same period clothing appeared in a mist. He seemed to be searching for something, too. Could the spirits have been searching for each other or a certain object?

As a neighbor boy was walking his dog late one night, he saw a transparent man on the porch of the Riggs house. The boy informed the owner. Concerned that a previous owner may have died in the house, the resident researched the house's history. He discovered that nearly one hundred years ago, his house was owned by the Baptist minister Reverend Norman Hough, who lived in the house into the 1920s. Aware of a possible haunting, the homeowner became astutely aware of the strange and unexplainable things that occurred around the home. The front door would open by itself, a rocking chair would rock of its own accord, and the curtains in the living room would fly away from the wall whenever someone walked past them. The homeowner would retire for the night and wake the next morning to discover every mirror that had been hanging on the wall was on the floor, leaning against the wall, unbroken. Since mirrors are thought to be portals, could the religious Reverend Hough be responsible for taking them off the walls?

So, who is haunting this historic house—Henry and Martha Riggs, Reverend Norman Hough, or all three?

THE FENTON BAPTIST SEMINARY

In 1863, Mrs. Rosina L. Dayfoot, the wife of Reverend Peter Dayfoot, was the schoolmaster of the town's original Baptist private school. With the population of Fentonville increasing, Reverend and Mrs. Dayfoot recognized the need to have a larger building for educating the children. They began working diligently to raise money to build a school to offer additional private education. David L. Latourette, a local banker, donated a portion of land, which was enclosed by High and Seminary Streets and State Road. He also gave a substantial monetary contribution toward the construction of the building. A wooden structure was built on the west side of the property to temporarily accommodate Dayfoot's ever-expanding class size. With additional funds from the Baptist church and other community members, the cornerstone for the Fenton Baptist Seminary building, located at 305 High Street on the corner of State Road, was laid on June 17, 1869.

The auspicious day was overseen by Reverend Thomas Jefferson Joslin, who dedicated the cornerstone with the following words:

> *And today, we meet to place in position, with simple but solemn and becoming service, the cornerstone of a temple designed to promote Christian education. Within its well-wrought chest, you will soon deposit a few records, a list of names and some pictures on which as decades fill their round years the eyes of men will be cast with an interest ever fresh and ever increasing. Some of you who rank as joint founders of this institution, and*

The Fenton Baptist Seminary. *Fenton Historical Society.*

who bring novel sacrifices to its altars, will come possibly a time or two to review these deposits, and then to your children and to generations following, they shall be mementos of you, and of this age, and this day, and of this very hour, and of the friends now gathered with you here. But what is better still, you will complete this temple, you will dedicate its halls, you will place the workmen at their posts, you will unfold science and point the way to God. And thus, advancing the columns of humanity, you hasten the solution of the problem of the union of the race in the "one God and Father of all." And to him who queries, be it known that these stones signify receding darkness and advancing light.

Once the ten-thousand-square-foot building was completed, the first gathering held within its walls was a wake and tribute to Rosina Dayfoot, who passed away just shy of its opening.

For twenty years, the Fenton Baptist Seminary was a private feeder school for Kalamazoo College. The students who chose to prepare themselves for college there could enter the school without taking an exam. The Fenton Baptist Seminary housed the boys on the first floor, the second floor was used for study, and the girls roomed on the third floor. It offered many courses of study—normal, classical, English/scientific, science, Latin/scientific, business, gym, and music. With the competition of Fenton's public schools growing in strength, the private school closed in 1888 and became a retirement home for Baptist ministers and a home to widows and small children. In 1899, a gasoline stove exploded, causing the building to burn. The residents were evacuated safely. When the fire was extinguished, only the stone walls remained. Reconstructed around 1900, the facility again became a retirement home.

One of its retirees was Reverend Henry St. Claire and his wife, Marion. They enjoyed their retirement years in the Fenton Baptist Seminary and resided in one of its fifteen rooms. Reverend St. Claire passed away on January 11, 1908, at the age of eighty-four. His wife, wanting to earn her keep, took on the responsibility of tending to the retirement home's chickens and became known as Auntie St. Clair, the chicken lady. She passed away on March 16, 1927, at the age of seventy-nine. The couple rests in peace, side by side, in a reserved area for the past residents of the Fenton Baptist Seminary in section B of Oakwood Cemetery. There is a large granite marker, the cornerstone of the building, and a memorial bench within Fenton Baptist Seminary's reserved site.

Another resident of the Fenton Baptist Seminary was Reverend Edward A. Abbott. He was born in Wisconsin in 1846. In 1864, when he was eighteen years old, he tried to enlist in the Union army. Abbott was denied entry because his father and three brothers were already enlisted, and he was needed on the family's farm. One of his brothers died in the notorious Andersonville Prison, where Union prisoners survived only a short time

The Fenton Baptist Seminary fire. *Fenton Historical Society.*

under horrid conditions. Edward Abbott traveled to Kansas and became a Baptist preacher and sheriff. He married Sara Jane Schooley in 1872, returned to his hometown in Wisconsin, and continued his career as a minister. In 1900, the couple separated for reasons of incompatibility. Sara went to Los Angeles, and Edward traveled to Montana, where he ranched until 1920, when he moved to North Dakota. He lived the last of his days in the Fenton Baptist Seminary and passed away in 1932, well over the age of eighty.

The retirement home closed its doors sometime in the 1930s. It was sold and used for several purposes until it became the Hilltop Nursing Home. A paperboy, who had the nursing home on his route, tried to avoid stepping inside the building. He said, "It was scary. The people would stare at me mindlessly and walk toward me like zombies and want to touch me. When forced to go inside, I always made my visit as short as possible." The nursing home was closed in 1967. It remained vacant until the mid-1990s, when it was purchased by an individual who intended to restore the building. After some research, the new owner learned of a safe that was in a wall fifteen feet above ground. Assuming it was the cornerstone, she and her son discovered it behind several layers of wallpaper, plaster, and slat boards. Once the safe was opened, it revealed old newspapers, letters, and three catalogues documenting the three years prior to the construction of the building. The catalogues, the oldest dated 1865–66, listed the names of the school's doners, along with the amount they donated, photographs, autographs of the ministers and teachers, and copies of the *Fenton Independent* newspaper. However, the photographs were not in the safe. Bits of charred wood surrounded the safe, which indicated it survived the fire of February 21, 1899. The owner featured a "haunted house" within the building's walls until it was cited by the City of Fenton to discontinue due to the lack of proper permits and safety issues.

A circulated story tells of a group of young men who entered the dark building one night. One of them threw an empty plastic drink bottle through the open doorway of a vacant room, only to have it thrown back at him. Those who dared to spend the night spoke of creaks, strange noises, and doors that opened and closed by themselves. One of the visitors reported seeing a rocking chair rock of its own accord. The curious explorers left and never returned.

The aged building suffered damage from a storm in 2013, causing a section of the front wall to fall away in 2014. As a result, the building was condemned and demolished in 2015. Some who visit the empty lot report an uneasy feeling with each step they take. Photographs they have taken during nightly visits often show orbs or distortedly glowing lines and shadows. With a good number of retired residents passing away on the property over the years, could their residual energies believe the building is still there?

THE LATOURETTE FAMILY

W hen Howard Booth LaTourette wed Ella Wallbridge Sheldon, they brought together four legendary Fenton families: the LeRoys, the Booths, the Sheldons and the LaTourettes. These four families were major contributors to the growth and development of Fenton.

Ella's father was Deacon Robert Livingston Sheldon, born in Herkimer, New York. He married Sarah LeRoy, also born in New York. She was the daughter of Judge Daniel LeRoy and Edith Wallbridge Fobes. The couple moved from New York to Pontiac, Michigan, in 1830 and then to Fenton in 1846. Robert and Sarah owned and operated the local dry goods store there. They were active in both the political and religious communities of the town. Robert served as the city treasurer for many years. The barn on their property was a station on the Underground Railroad, which helped escaped enslaved people on their journeys toward Canada and freedom. When Robert expected enslaved people to arrive, he instructed his family, "Don't go into the barn tonight." The escaped enslaved people would leave early the next morning for the next station.

Judge Daniel LeRoy married Edith "Ede" Walbridge Fobes in 1799. He was one of the original purchasers of land in what is now Pontiac, Michigan. Upon settling in Michigan in 1819, he was appointed prosecuting attorney for the area. He was the U.S. district attorney from 1826 to 1830. He served as the postmaster general before being appointed attorney of the United States in and for the territory of Michigan by President John Quincy Adams, and he served in this position from 1830 to 1831. He was also the president

The Joining of the LaTourette, LeRoy, Booth, and Sheldon Families

David LaTourette 1778 – 1852	Hannah Hegeman 1790 – 1868		Reverend John Booth 1796 – 1869	Lady Jane Anne Wisdom 1799 – 1862		Judge Daniel LeRoy 1775 – 1858	Edith Wallbridge Fobes 1781 – 1848

David Louis LaTourette 1823 – 1885

Emma Matilda Booth 1824 – 1908

Deacon Robert Livingston Sheldon 1805 – 1871

Sarah LeRoy 1811 – 1891

Howard Booth LaTourette 1847 – 1906

Ella Wallbridge Sheldon 1848 – 1915

The LaTourette family tree. *Brenda Hasse.*

elector for Michigan in 1836 and the Michigan state attorney general from 1836 to 1837. His daughter was quoted as saying, "Judge LeRoy was absent from home a great deal, engaged on the various duties connected with the offices he held and spent much time in Washington. He was well educated and spoke French fluently. For that reason, he was selected as envoy to Cuba by the president."

While Judge Daniel LeRoy was well known and respected, it is Sarah's brother Robert who is best remembered for his participation in purchasing Dibbleville from Clark Dibble and playing the poker game with Colonel William Fenton and Benjamin Rockwell on August 24, 1837.

Howard's parents were David Louis LaTourette and Emma Matilda Booth. Emma was the daughter of Reverend John Booth and Lady Jane Wisdom, who was a descendant of Irish royalty. The Reverend John and Lady Jane brought their growing family to the Fentonville area. The reverend was of the Baptist faith. He was said to be a "highly esteemed clergyman" who organized the building of a hall on Leroy Street, the congregation's first permanent home, and was responsible for two extensions to the town's plat. Reverend John Booth and his wife, Lady Jane Wisdom, were both buried in Old Prospect Hill in Oakwood Cemetery. Howard's father, David Lewis LaTourette, was known as the "character" in the family. He was born in New York and married Emma in 1845, when he was twenty-two years old. Howard and his sister were born in Michigan, but by 1850, the family of four had moved to St. Louis, Missouri, where David founded, owned, and operated a linseed and castor oil business. The business grew substantially and was quite profitable. He sold it nine years later, in 1859, for a handsome sum and moved his wife and four children back to Fentonville. David built a large stone house on a farm in Tyrone Hills.

David LaTourette opened the First National Bank of Fenton in 1863. The former bank was located at 104 South Leroy Street, the current location of Bridge Street Exchange, a men's clothing store. Adjoining his bank was the Baptist Hall, in which Mrs. Rosina L. Dayfoot would teach school. David was the main stockholder of the Fenton Manufacturing Company in 1864. He was an active member of the Fenton Baptist Seminary Board of Trustees and donated the land and made a substantial financial contribution to the seminary's construction in 1868. In the 1870 U.S. census, David LaTourette's personal estate was valued at $100,000. Local history described him in the following way: "He was the most influential moneyed man in the region. He seems to be a friend of every charitable institution and contributes largely of his means every year." A year later, he owned and controlled banks in Fenton and Grand Rapids.

What truly happened to David LaTourette? The family would like to believe that David's health began to deteriorate in the autumn of 1871. He turned his businesses over to his son Howard before leaving Fenton with his wife and youngest children and moving to Arkansas. However, there is much more to his story.

Author Albert Baxter, who wrote *The History of the City of Grand Rapids* in 1891, indicates,

> *In 1870, David L. LaTourette instituted a branch in this city of his bank in Fenton. He was heralded by sundry persons, immensely no doubt, as a man of abundant means, great liberality, honorable in his dealings and likely to prove a permanent acquisition to the business circles. He soon adopted unusual and unsafe methods of conducting banking by offering extraordinary rates of interest upon deposits. Prudent and cautious persons avoided his institution, but many fell into his traps, and within two years, he succeeded in getting into his possession not less than $75,000 of the hard earnings of our poorer citizens. Secretly, he left the city. His after record was a sad one. The dividends received by the Grand Rapids creditors were only nominal.*

The book *The History of Genesee County Michigan* describes his bank failure:

> *The First National Bank of Fenton was organized in the summer of 1963 by David L. LaTourette as president and manager. He also established*

a bank at Grand Rapids. In 1872, affairs having been for some time indicating that serious changes were about to take place, the culminating point was reached—LaTourette failed, the bank was closed, the operations of the woolen factory were suspended, and stockholders suffered severe losses. Many were disposed to blame Mr. LaTourette, and others were more lenient. The circumstances are well known to the citizens.

With his parents and siblings absent, Howard remained behind in Fenton with the responsibility of picking up the financial fragments left by his father. He opened the Commerce State Bank and repaid any debts David had left.

Howard Booth LaTourette was born on May 7, 1847. An article under the heading "Local Lies, Legends, and Lore" appeared in the *Fenton Independent* newspaper on October 14, 1971, describing Howard's adventure as an infant:

Mrs. David LaTourette was on her front porch, shucking peas and rocking baby Howard's cradle with her foot. An Indian squaw stealthily emerged from the thicket. She proceeded to Howard's cradle, took her own papoose from her back, removed Howard and made an exchange of babies. With Howard secured on her back, she vanished into the woods. All of this was viewed with indifference by Mrs. LaTourette, who continued to shuck her peas. After an hour elapsed and the imperturbable Mrs. LaTourette was still shucking peas, the squaw again appeared through the thicket. She walked to the cradle and returned Howard, then took her own baby back, breaking into compulsive laughter, a rare thing. The white woman's strength of character had been tested by the Indian. She had gained respect and dignity.

Despite his father, Howard and his family were wealthy and well respected. Howard, Ella, and their seven children were musicians; they were active in the community and well educated. Only two of their children stayed in Fenton through most of their adult lives. Lou, their second daughter, never married and served for more than twenty years as the superintendent of the Old Baptist Retirement Home, formerly the Fenton Baptist Seminary. She was affectionately known by all as Sister Lou. Sheldon, their second-youngest son, also stayed on in Fenton. He owned and operated a farm, was active in government, announced the morning farm report on the radio, and was instrumental in establishing the

4-H Club in Fenton. However, residents may best remember how Sheldon announced the end of winter. He would walk to the end of his dock, take off all his clothes, and jump into the lake. He called it "spring fling." This was done much to the amusement and abhorrence of his neighbors.

Think what you may of David LaTourette, but he provided for his family and helped others escape to freedom.

Andrew J. Phillips's Factory, House, and Personal Office

Andrew J. Phillips was one of Fenton's most notable and prominent residents of his time. His business, the A.J. Phillips Factory, once led the state of Michigan in manufacturing.

Phillips was born in Hartland Township, Michigan, in a log house on October 9, 1837. He was one of seven children. His education entailed attending a log schoolhouse until he was seventeen. He continued his education at Union School in Milford, Michigan. Phillips began working as a pump maker in Calhoun County at the age of twenty. He helped improve the manufacturing process of the pump. After his marriage to Julia Anna Bullard in 1862, he moved to Milford and began working in partnership with the Wells brothers in manufacturing reapers and mowers. When the Civil War began, the iron and steel supply became limited. He sold his share of the partnership. Pulling from his manufacturing education, Phillips cut down tamarack trees and bored and produced wooden pumps. In 1869, he moved to Fenton and purchased a three-story brick building on the northwest corner of Leroy and Mill Streets, where the Fenton Post Office is currently located at 210 South Leroy Street. Phillips continued to manufacture wooden pumps, and his family resided on the second floor of the building. He began growing his business and purchased steam power. Sometime in the early 1880s, Phillips invented the adjustable window screen. It was a popular product in 1884, with

Andrew Jackson Phillips. *Fenton Historical Society.*

Top: A.J. Phillips factory, 1900. *Fenton Historical Society*.

Bottom: A.J. Phillips factory employees, 1895. *Fenton Historical Society*.

Opposite: Andrew Jackson Phillips with his wife, Julia Anna Bullard Phillips, and sons, Winfield Byron, Edward Ashley and Harry Judson. *Fenton Historical Society*.

the local paper announcing the sale of over 1,200 screens to one buyer and 2,400 for the year. It has been said that the White House in Washington, D.C., installed Phillips's window screens. In 1888, Andrew's brother Charles and two of his three sons, Winfield B. and Edward Ashley, joined the company. The manufacturing company changed its name and was now known as A.J. Phillips and Company. It expanded its line of products to include milk safes. Phillips invented the first wooden bent steel-edge snow shovel by boiling the wood in his kitchen and clamping it to a form until it dried. He sold over 75,000 bent wooden snow shovels a year.

With his business flourishing, Phillips needed to expand. He acquired more land and buildings until A.J. Phillips and Company covered three and a half acres of floor space and twelve acres of land. Phillips constructed two buildings, one that was 26,000 square feet and another that was four stories tall. In total, his buildings included over fifty thousand square feet of floor space. His factory employed seventy-five to one hundred men and shipped products to every state of the Union. Sales of products exceeded $150,000 annually. To produce the products, over 1.5 million square feet of wire screen and 3 to 4 million feet of lumber was used annually. The company also employed traveling salesmen.

Phillips's motto was, "Not how much, but how well," and he prided himself on the quality of his manufactured products. The company produced a catalog of over forty items for sale. Phillips's third son, Harry Judson Phillips, joined the company in 1894. The Sanborn fire map of 1895 indicates Phillips was using a small building located at 300 South Leroy Street, at the southwest corner of Leroy and Mill Streets, as his business office. Phillips also had a free library that his employees could use.

RESIDENCE

In 1891, Phillips built his house at the northwest corner of Adelaide Street and Shiawassee Avenue. It was constructed with a solid foundation and walls made from tamarack wood that was horizontally spiked together to barricade mice from entering the house. The elegant stairway to the second floor is embellished with the finest of wood. The tall ceilings draw one's eyes upward to take in each room's vastness. The paneled wooden pocket doors close off rooms for privacy. A ballroom is located on the third floor.

Andrew Jackson Phillips's grand residence on West Shiawassee Avenue. *Fenton Historical Society.*

Personal Office

Mrs. Julia Phillips began using her husband's business office to hold meetings for the Women's Christian Temperance Movement. Her husband was less than pleased, especially since he liked to partake in an adult beverage from time to time. In 1900, Mr. Phillips built a private office where the Riggs Hotel once stood. Temperance meetings were not tolerated within its walls. On June 4, 1904, Andrew J. Phillips passed away. His private office was willed to the city of Fenton under three conditions: (1) the building must be well maintained, both inside and outside; (2) the building would be used as a library, and the only meetings held within its walls must have a library agenda—no temperance meetings were allowed; and (3) a board of trustees would be appointed by the village council to oversee the library's operation. Phillips bequeathed $500 to provide books for the library. It remained the A.J. Phillips Library until 1987, when the library relocated to the former post office on the corner of Caroline and Walnut Streets. The building has been transformed into the A.J. Phillips Fenton Museum. The Fenton Historical Society has its office located in one of the building's small rooms, and it maintains a Fenton history library for research.

In the second-story center window of the A.J. Phillips Fenton Museum, the apparition of Marjorie Marshall Phillips can often be seen dressed in a white gown and clutching a teddy bear in the crook of her arm. Marjorie, the granddaughter of A.J. Phillips, passed away at the age of seven.

Visitors to the former A.J. Phillips Business Office, currently Yesterday's Treasures Antique Shop, experience Mrs. Phillips's presence. Some say

Left: A.J. Phillips Fenton Library. *Fenton Historical Society*.

Right: A.J. Phillips Fenton Museum. *Brenda Hasse*.

Andrew Jackson Phillips's grandchildren. Marjorie is front, center. *Fenton Historical Society*.

she stands in the northern picture window and wipes her tears with a handkerchief. Is she upset because she knows her husband is hiding in his private office, indulging in his favorite beverage?

Phillips Row

West Shiawassee Avenue is one of the main residential streets in Fenton, and it is lined with historic houses. The Cheney log cabin was one of the first houses built in Dibbleville. It was located on the northwest corner of West Shiawassee Avenue and Adelaide Street. The second house to be built on the budding street was located at 218 West Shiawassee Avenue in 1867. In 1878, Josiah Buckbee built an impressive Victorian-style house at 308 West Shiawassee Avenue. He was a prominent businessman and banker. The home was later owned by Charles Damon, also known as "Left-Handed Charlie." He was a sharpshooter and traveled with the Wild West shows. He was also the founder of the Fenton Historical Society. Andrew Jackson Phillips's house, built in 1891 on the land where the Cheney log cabin once resided at 202 West Shiawassee Avenue, is distinct, impressive, and a clear indication of Phillips's vast wealth, with its Queen Anne–style architecture. Phillips went on to build a house for each of his three sons. His oldest son, Winfield, owned the beautiful house at 404 West Shiawassee Avenue. The house, built by Colonel William Fenton, was moved to West Street, and a house for Edward Ashley was constructed in its place. This magnificent one-and-a-half-story house, with its stone façade and siding, includes a lovely barn. It is located at 304 West Shiawassee Avenue. In 1904, Harry Phillips, the youngest of the three sons, received an equally impressive house with colonial pillars located at 214 West Shiawassee Avenue. Like ducks in a row, the Phillips family's houses were nicknamed "Phillips Row."

Andrew Jackson Phillips passed away in his majestic home. Some who enter his former residence walk from room to room and believe his spirit still resides within his house and they feel as if they are being watched. Perhaps A.J. Phillips is proud of his accomplishments from his physical life and is honored others are admiring what he built, which is standing the test of time.

Even though the Phillips family has a mausoleum in section G of Oakwood Cemetery, Andrew Phillips's remains are absent. Since it was constructed after his passing, his grave is located nearby.

CEMENTVILLE

Traveling west from Fenton by way of Silver Lake Road, Detroit firms purchased land in 1900 on two lakes: Silver Lake and Lake Ponemah, which was formerly known as Mud Lake. On the south side of the road, the firms built two cement plants: the Aetna Portland Cement Plant, which opened in 1902, and the Egyptian Portland Cement Plant, which opened in 1903. The two were separated by the railroad tracks running between them. A steam shovel attached to a wooden dredge would harvest marl from the bottom of the lakes. Marl, made of clay and silt, was the main ingredient of cement. The shovel would place it in scows, flat-bottom boats with squared-off ends used to transport bulk material. The tugboat *Oscar I* pulled the loaded barges to pumping stations to unload the silt.

A suction tube and pipe carried the marl to the plant for processing. The marl was put through a wet grind and crushed into a fine powder. Clay and other ingredients were added and pumped into eight large coal-fired kilns. What emerged from the kiln were known as "clinkers." The clinkers had gypsum added to them before they were ground into cement. The product was combined with clay to make the best grade of cement and put into barrels. The cement was also bagged into sacks weighing one hundred pounds each. The dredging of the lakes caused them to nearly double in size. The dredging also created Lake Tupper off Lake Ponemah and Marl Lake off Silver Lake. The small community around the lakes was nicknamed Cementville.

Harvesting marl from the lake. *Fenton Historical Society*.

The Aetna Portland Cement factory. *Fenton Historical Society*.

The Jitney Bus transporting cement workers to the cement plants. *Fenton Historical Society*.

The Aetna Portland Cement plant was nestled on the edge of Lake Ponemah on the old Woodruff farm, which was over eighty acres in size. The plant cost over $500,000 to build and used seven hundred thousand bricks in its construction. Two giant generators supplied the plant with electricity. Its daily average production was one thousand bags of cement. At peak production, the plant employed two hundred men on two shifts and operated twenty-four hours a day, seven days a week. A loud whistle could be heard at seven o'clock in the morning and seven o'clock in the evening, indicating the start and end of the workday.

Men would ride bicycles, forming a pathway over time, or hop on a horse-drawn bus for their workday transportation. The bus could carry over one dozen men at a time to the plant. The plant was closed during the winter months because the lakes would freeze, making it impossible to harvest the marl. The president of Aetna was Earl Bunce. He lived at 210 High Street in the 1920s.

The Egyptian Portland Cement plant was located on the edge of Silver Lake. The Detroit firm paid J.P.C. Riggs $45,000 for the property, and the plant's construction cost approximately $300,000. The plant began producing cement in the summer of 1903. Carlos Shotwell was the secretary of Egyptian and lived at 812 South Adelaide Street.

Egyptian Portland Cement Works. *Fenton Historical Society*.

The plants' excellent railroad station was known as West Fenton. It took three flatcars to transport the company's rotary clinker heater to the cement plant for installation. The oven was eighty-five feet long.

Working at the plants was hard and laborious. It had its dangers, too. In 1903, Patrick Cuff worked at the Aetna Plant. He was an oiler on the night shift. His clothing was caught on a bolt in a revolving shaft, and he was whirled and smashed to death. Another death occurred when an explosion ripped through the coal room. Another man was entangled in a shaft that crushed marl while another worker was scalded to death when a tube from a boiler exploded. Many of the workers were of Hungarian descent and brought in from Detroit. In 1906, their pay was twenty-five cents per day.

The cement used to pave the first road in the United States was supplied by the Egyptian Portland Cement Plant and the Aetna Portland Cement Plant. Exactly one mile of Woodward Avenue was paved between Seven Mile and Eight Mile Roads in Detroit. It was proudly stamped "Made in Fenton."

The Egyptian Portland Cement Plant was closed in 1920.

The Aetna Portland Cement Plant shifted its dredging operation to Silver Lake after moving the tugboat and scows and building a pumping station on the northwest shore of the lake. The marl was transported through an underground pipe. A channel was dug between Silver Lake and a small lake that was named Marl Lake. The tugboat made four round trips between the two lakes per day.

With limestone being an easier and less expensive additive to obtain, it replaced marl in the 1930s. The Aetna Portland Cement Plant closed in 1936. A longtime Aetna employee was quoted as saying, "We knew the end was coming. Then one day, the plant was closed."

THE ST. AMAND SCANDAL

Caroline LeRoy, the sister of Robert LeRoy and daughter of Judge Daniel LeRoy, was born on March 6, 1816, in Binghamton, Broome County, New York. The LeRoy family settled in Pontiac, Michigan. Her brother Robert and Colonel William M. Fenton purchased Dibbleville from Clark Dibble in 1836.

One afternoon, Judge LeRoy and Caroline traveled southward on the Saginaw Turnpike, near Springfield, heading for their home in Pontiac after visiting family in Fenton. Today, the Saginaw Turnpike is known as Dixie Highway. Unfortunately, their carriage broke down. Since Judge LeRoy was unable to make the necessary repairs by himself, they were stranded. They discovered they were surrounded by wilderness, home to various wild animals and perhaps a nearby Native village. They did not have to wait long before a very handsome man who was traveling in the opposite direction reined his horse to stop his wagon before them. Augustus St. Amand hopped down from his seat and helped Judge LeRoy make the necessary repairs to the carriage. Caroline was impressed by the gallant gentleman. She considered his gesture chivalric, too. She thought it strange that he remained silent while he worked. He only spoke when they departed: "Au revoir."

Augustus St. Amand came to this country from Paris, France, after inheriting one-third of $1 million. He arrived in New Orleans, traveled up the Mississippi River, purchased a plot of land from a friend on Byram Lake and built a log cabin. He was traveling from Detroit after obtaining supplies when he encountered the gentleman and his daughter in distress.

Left: Augustus St. Amand. *Fenton Historical Society*.

Below: 206 Rockwell Street. *Brenda Hasse*.

He may have searched his heart after meeting Caroline and sought her father's permission to court her, because they were wed in Fentonville on February 5, 1839.

They moved into the house located at 206 Rockwell Street shortly after it was built by Caroline's brother and Colonel Fenton in 1842. It had only four rooms then—two downstairs and two upstairs. The couple was blessed with four children during their eight years of marriage. Their son, Augustus, served for the United States and died of typhoid fever during the Civil War. Their other children were Fernenard, Leroy, and Caroline Emma. Eleven days after giving birth to little Caroline Emma, Caroline passed away in one of the upstairs bedrooms on April 12, 1847, at the age of thirty-one. Caroline Emma died three months later. Caroline was buried in the family plot in Old Prospect Hill, the oldest section of Oakwood Cemetery. The engraving on her headstone is written in French and reads, "Here rests Caroline St. Amand born the 6th of March 1816, good daughter, virtuous wife, excellent mother, she died a good Christian on the 12th of April 1847." It is assumed Caroline Emma lies in rest next to her mother, although her marker is either missing or was never made.

Emily Steere was visiting friends in Fenton when she was introduced to Augustus. They were married in May 1848, just over a year after the passing of Caroline. The St. Amands lived in Flint. Their household was blessed by the birth of their daughter, Caroline Emily, on May 20, 1859. Emily was left with all four children and one on the way when Augustus abruptly left his job as the treasurer for Genesee County in 1851. Before he left for France on urgent business, he told Emily of his lonely childhood, detailing his attendance at a convent as a child and saying he rarely saw his parents, even though they lived nearby. Shortly after his departure, the township's books were discovered to be out of balance. Robert L. Sheldon and Colonel William Fenton replaced the missing funds with their own money. Augustus apparently left the country to try to obtain the remainder of his inheritance from a reverend in the convent where he was educated. During Augustus's absence abroad, rumors reached Emily's ears that her husband had lost his money through bad investments of land. Emily received no communication or letters the entire time Augustus was abroad. Throughout her pregnancy, Emily worried about Augustus and constantly wondered if he would ever return. When he finally returned home, he was emptyhanded. The clerk at the convent told him the reverend had confiscated the remainder of his inheritance—or at least it was the excuse he gave his wife. Their son Earnest was born in December 1851. Because of her worried state during Augustus's absence, Emily blamed the child's poor health on her husband. The family moved to Wallsville, Pennsylvania, shortly after Augustus's return from abroad.

Augustus St. Amund passed away in 1883. Emily Steere St. Amund died in 1886. They both lay in rest in Shoemaker Cemetery in Dalton, Lackawanna County, Pennsylvania.

WILLIAMS AVIATION SCHOOL

Orville and Wilbur Wright flew their plane *Flyer* in Kitty Hawk, North Carolina, in 1903. Just over a decade later, Osbert E. Williams, an aviator and barnstormer, came to Fenton.

OSBERT E. WILLIAMS

Osbert E. Williams, or, as many knew him, Bert, was born in Webster, Michigan, to a farming family. During a time when steam power and steam engines were important tools to farmers, fixing them when they broke down became second nature to Osbert. His mechanical skills led him away from the farm and to Ypsilanti, where he focused on engineering. He then moved to Scranton, Pennsylvania. In March 1904, he married Inez Augusta Blessing, an instructor for the International Correspondence School in Scranton. She taught electrical engineering. Their son Ralph was born a year later. They had three other children: Robert, Sarah, and Grace. Only Ralph and Sarah lived to adulthood. In 1907, while overseeing the powerhouse for the Laurel Line Railroad, an electric streetcar commuter system in Scranton, Williams became interested in early aviation development and began studying everything he could find on the subject. Williams worked for the Westinghouse Company that was based in Pittsburg, Pennsylvania, during the project. He was later hired by the railroad.

Williams Aviation School. *Fenton Historical Society.*

A sidestep in his career took him to Spring City, Pennsylvania, to work during the construction of Penn Hurst, as we know it today. After the completion of the project, Williams went to Detroit and became an engineer on watch for the Detroit Edison Company. He returned to Scranton, gave up his career and chased his passion to establish the Williams Aeroplane Company, which would build airplanes that resembled tinker toy models, and begin a flight school. His company became known as the first Scranton-based aviation enterprise. He also performed aeronautical stunts at state and county fairs.

Williams then traveled to Fenton, Michigan, to repair a hydroplane owned by Mr. Armstrong, a wealthy Flint sportsman with a summer home on Long Lake, now known as Lake Fenton. He was so impressed with the city, he purchased a building on South Leroy Street, just north of the Shiawassee River and south of today's Fenton Community Center. Most likely, the building was the vacant Roc Manufacturing Company building, which once made whip sockets. He moved his family and business to Fenton and began manufacturing airplanes. A flat piece of land at the north end of Lake Fenton was used as his landing strip. As he took off and landed from his airstrip, it attracted the attention of curious young men. He offered rides to the bystanders, which soon caused them to take interest in learning to fly; thus began the Williams Aviation School.

The water rat. *Fenton Historical Society.*

Flying students. *Fenton Historical Society.*

The school's first plane was nicknamed the "water rat" because it took off and landed on the surface of the water. Williams soon added several land planes to the school.

The planes used in the Williams Aviation School were described as having "flimsy construction," with an exposed frame and no fuselage. The motor was small and often stopped while the plane was in flight. The propeller was composed of several pieces of wood that were glued and pressed together. The rib and strut constructions were often held together with hay wire to strengthen the connection joints. The flying machines were considered state-of-the-art for their time. However, they were not guaranteed to stay together during a flight and often fell apart.

Williams was the main attraction of the Patterson Aviators, a group that was put together by John T. Patterson of Detroit. The Patterson Aviators were temporarily sworn in as the first U.S. mail carriers and airmail carriers.

WILLIAMS AVIATORS

Word of the school soon reached nearby cities and attracted adventurous young men to join. Two such men were Al Boshek and Cyrus Bettis, who both mastered the art of flying. They offered thrilling rides to passengers. If their plane rattled during a flight, they would return to the ground to rewire the loose joints before resuming and completing the flight. Boshek left the school and performed his defying flying skills at county fairs. He later died in an accident that occurred while he was stunt flying in Holdridge, Nebraska.

The school's student body increased to one dozen. One student was First Lieutenant John Thad Johnson. He was considered a hero to many, but in truth, he lived his life doing what he loved to do most: flying. He was born in Johnson City, Texas, on July 19, 1893, studied at the Theological School at Trinity University in Waxahachie, Texas, and was a Presbyterian clergyman in Dallas before enlisting in the army at the age of twenty-three.

Johnson was an amateur at flying, but he owned his own flying machine. Once in the Signal Corps, he came to Fenton to receive additional training at the Williams Aviator School. Stationed at Selfridge Field, he was commissioned first lieutenant of the infantry in 1917 and transferred in August to the signal corps at Rockwell Field, California, to begin his training as a military aviator. From there, Johnson was sent to France and served in active duty on the European front during World War I.

In 1919, Johnson participated in a transcontinental race. On November 18 that year, he married Edith N. Naylor before being stationed in Hawaii. Unfortunately, her health suffered greatly in the tropical climate. In 1923, the couple returned to the mainland, where Edith passed away.

In September 1924, Johnson was a contender for the John L. Michael Trophy Race, which was to take place on October 4 at Selfridge. However, the trophy was awarded to a pilot who flew the fastest at just under 217 miles per hour.

Johnson's squadron tried to set distance records, too. They attempted to fly from Selfridge to San Antonio, Texas, in one day, but rain caused them to fall short of their goal. In March 1925, twelve planes left Selfridge, headed for Camp Wheeler in Miami, Florida. Unfortunately, Johnson's plane had complications and was forced to land in Gray, Georgia. One of his more perilous flights occurred on April 19, when Johnson flew from Selfridge to Washington, D.C. He was over Pennsylvania, near Eagle Mere, when he encountered a heavy storm. Johnson could see oil sputtering from his engine. He tried to continue the flight, but his engine failed. He looked over the side of the plane and could not see the ground. He had no other choice than to abandon his craft, so he jumped. Unknown to Johnson, he was ten thousand feet from the ground. His jump was the longest leap ever attempted by a pilot, and it set a record.

On October 24, Johnson married Mildred Faye Adams of Fenton. The ceremony was performed at 612 South Adelaide Street, where Mildred's parents, Henry and Victoria Adams, resided.

On July 7, 1926, Johnson was one of three pilots who escorted the second commercial airplane reliability tour from Detroit to Saint Paul, Minnesota. In mid-September, Johnson played a role in filming the movie *Wings* near San Antonio. He was assigned one of twelve biplanes to fly. He guided his plane through several dives and bombings over a set of a French village while he was filmed from the ground. A cameraman came along for the ride and filmed the village from above, too. Johnson indicated the cameraman's face looked a little green when they landed.

In July 1927, a big celebration was planned in Canada for Ottawa's diamond jubilee celebration, in which Johnson accompanied the guest of honor, Colonel Charles L. Lindbergh. Lindbergh arrived at Selfridge ahead of Johnson and the other pilots. Once again, Johnson flew a biplane. There were twelve planes escorting *The Spirit of St. Louis* to the event on July 3. As the hum of the plane's engines echoed from the sky, the gathered crowd looked upward to see Charles Lindbergh leading the V-shaped formation.

The lead pilot dipped the nose of his plane, and the others followed in a high-speed descent as the formation headed for the crowd. Unaccustomed to the exhibition, the people panicked and scattered as the planes came within a few hundred feet of them before climbing skyward again. Lindbergh landed his plane first, smooth as butter. Seven of the planes landed safely. Johnson went to land, but the nose of his plane rose unexpectedly, as if it wanted to resume its position in the air. The pilot behind him ran into the tail of Johnson's plane, forcing him upward. The crowd watched as Johnson's plane's tail section fell from the sky. He struggled to get out of his seat, but he managed to jump. Since he was only one hundred feet above the ground, his parachute was unable to break his fall. He landed on his shoulder and head and died instantly. The authorities roped off the totaled plane, but they could not hold back members of the curious crowd as they gathered to view the wreckage. Even Lindbergh stood silently. His face, normally smiling, was solemn throughout the remainder of the event.

Johnson was the commanding officer of the Twenty-Seventh Squadron Selfridge Field Fliers, one of the oldest officers at the time. He served ten years in the U.S. Army Air Service and five years at Selfridge Field. The cause of death on his certificate says, "By mischance." Fellow pilots understood the true reason for the accident. It was prop wash, a churning of air by the aircraft that landed before Johnson's plane.

The Canadian government and its people gave Johnson a grand, stately funeral. His casket was placed in parliament, draped with the Stars and Stripes, his captain's hat, and sword on top. Over fifty thousand people paid their respects as Johnson's body laid in state. As the casket was loaded onto the train, Lindbergh circled his plane above it three times and dropped great armfuls of crimson peonies that were gathered and placed on the casket before it was transported from Ottawa to Fenton by train. Lindbergh and Johnson's fellow flying soldiers flew nearby throughout the trip. Out of respect, they cut their engines and dove silently until they were close to the train before rising again. Once in Fenton, Lindbergh waved his handkerchief out of his cockpit window as a final farewell before he headed back to Ottawa.

President Calvin Coolidge sent a wire to the prime minister, stating, "I deeply appreciate your heartfelt sympathy on the death of Lieutenant Johnson."

Back then, Fenton had a population of 2,500. Johnson was the seventh pilot from the Williams Aviation School in fourteen years to die. His funeral service was held at the First Presbyterian Church, with Reverend John Kitching presiding. Members of the Masonic Order, Selfridge Field men, intimate friends and family attended. Monsignor Patrick R. Dunnigan, the pastor of St. Michael's Church of Flint and a World War I chaplain, represented the army at the service.

Johnson served his country to the best of his ability and gave his life for the advancement of aviation.

Like Johnson, many of the Williams Aviation School students died trying to impress others with defying stunts. E.G. Knapp was the last school pilot to fall to his death in Texas in April 1928.

First Lieutenant John Thad Johnson was buried in Oakwood Cemetery in section B.

What Happened to Osbert E. Williams

In late 1916, Williams relocated his family and business to Mobile, Alabama. In October, as he was landing his plane at dusk, he could not see the ground and crashed. He succumbed to his injuries, leaving behind his wife, Ines; his son, Ralph; and his daughters, Sarah, and Grace. Inez moved her remaining family back to Scranton. She passed away in February 1920. Grace died in July 1921.

In a tribute to the pioneers in aviation, the Fenton Chamber of Commerce commemorated the life of Osbert Edwin Williams and his fellow aviators on Memorial Day 1929. Osbert E. Williams's name was the first of the twelve men recognized that day. It was dedicated "to the students of the Williams School of Aviation and others of our young men who gave their lives in the development of aviation."

THE AYRES HOUSE

This grand old house appears on the 1850 Genesee County map. Records indicate it was built in 1849 by Mr. and Mrs. Michael Ayres. Michael Ayers was born in Ireland and died in Fenton on March 27, 1867, at the age of eighty. Mary Callcutt Ayres was born in Oxfordshire, England, and died in Fentonville on October 3, 1853. Her age at the time of her death was unknown. They are both resting in peace in the Oakwood Cemetery in plot 217 of Old Prospect Hill.

The house in which they resided still exists today. It is located at 526 North Leroy Street. The original house was a basically structured two-story building made of brick. Their yard was enclosed by a decorative wire and white wooden fence, separating them from those who passed by on the plank sidewalk. The addition of the elegant pillar porch was added years later. Eventually, the residential property was zoned for commercial use and has housed several businesses over the years.

Those who have worked in the building have experienced many unexplained happenings. However, even though they became startled or frightened when strange things would occur, they believe the ghosts are friendly.

Office workers often pause in conversation and listen as heavy footsteps climb the stairs, followed by the sound of keys being dropped on the floor or on a table.

On another occasion, an employee, while working at her desk, heard people conversing in an adjoining room. When she entered the room to see who it was, no one was there.

Footsteps can often be heard upstairs, causing those on the first floor to look at the ceiling.

The sound of the front door opening caused one employee to rise from her desk to welcome whoever had entered the building. However, when she checked to see who was there, the employee discovered the room was empty and witnessed the front door open and close by itself.

On a busy day at the office, an employee answered the phone. The information she needed for the customer was in her car. She explained her reason for leaving for a few moments and placed the receiver on her desk before stepping away. When she returned, there was no one on the phone. She called the customer, who explained that a man had gotten on the line and said, "The woman had to leave and does not want to talk to you anymore." The employee was alone in the building at the time.

Could Mr. Ayres still believe he resides in his house? Does he watch over those who work within its walls? It appears he may come and go as he pleases and helps where he is needed, too.

113 MILL STREET

This former home on Mill Street once stood in the shadow of the A.J. Phillips Factory. It is listed as a dwelling on the 1859, 1884 and 1889 Sanborn Fire Insurance Maps. It appears as a rectangular structure with a front porch and small rectangular room attached to the back southeast corner on the 1859 and 1884 maps. On the 1889 map, two porches had been added to the back room. The house no longer exists, but those who resided within it remain. In 1960, a structure of cinderblocks was constructed, replacing the former home. The property may have been zoned for commercial use at that time.

When the Fenton Area Resource and Referral (FARR) store operated within the commercial building, its management and volunteers experienced strange happenings. Most of the paranormal activity was usually experienced when the store was closed and on Sundays. The following are a few examples of what the managers and volunteers endured.

Arriving at the building one Sunday, a manager was working in the basement when he heard a woman's voice call out, "Dinner's ready!" He went upstairs, assuming his wife had arrived with his lunch. Not finding her anywhere, he phoned home. She was busy making his lunch and had yet to leave their house.

Sometimes, voices would be heard in an adjoining room. When one of the volunteers went to investigate, no one was there.

A manager arrived one morning to use the copy machine before opening the store. While making copies, her name was called. After that, she refused to be in the store alone for a very long time.

After experiencing frequent strange occurrences, the managers contacted a medium, who explained the spirit was that of a woman. Her name was Elizabeth, and she once lived in a dwelling on the property. The medium then indicated Elizabeth was wearing an apron and removing something from an oven.

A frigid chill was often felt, as if someone had opened a window.

Anyone who visited FARR was aware of the rescued cats the managers would take in. Customers were usually greeted by the uncaged cats eager for a moment of their attention. The managers also housed kittens in the hopes someone would adopt them. One day, a volunteer watched from a short distance as a stuffed bear on top of a cat condo moved of its own accord. Both cats inside were sleeping. Was a spirit trying to play with the cats?

One of the store cats would often freeze in her tracks and look behind her. She refused to go into the basement by herself. When she was accompanied downstairs, the cat continued to act strangely, always watching, and snapping her head toward the slightest sound.

One evening, after closing the store, three women went to the basement and attempted to contact Elizabeth. The store cat accompanied them. When the women lit a candle and turned off the lights, the cat began to meow frantically. One of the women felt someone touch her neck.

A volunteer once left a gallon of paint and a paintbrush near the stairwell before going home for the night. When he went to retrieve it the next day, it was no longer there. He thought he may have left it at home, but when he returned home, it was not there. Going back to the store, he discovered the paint and paintbrush in the center of the basement floor. After inquiring with the managers and volunteers, everyone denied moving it.

Mechanical toys stored in the basement also began making noises by themselves. Some did not have batteries in them.

When a manager heard a resounding crash in an adjoining room, he entered and discovered an item on the floor. It had been on top of a television for many months. No one—not even one of the cats—was in the room. Was someone trying to get his attention?

One of the cats would become agitated and meow when the basement door was closed. The feline continued to make the annoying sound until someone opened the door. However, she would not go down the stairs once the door was open.

Automatic night lights would flash on and off for no apparent reason.

Even though Elizabeth's home no longer exists, her spirit lingers on the property. The property's current businesses suffered an unexplained fire on June 28, 2022. They have closed until further notice.

CYNTHIA ROBERTS GORTON, THE BLIND BARD OF MICHIGAN

C ynthis Roberts Gorton wrote under the pen name of Ida Glenwood. She was better known as the "Blind Bard of Michigan." The following is a poem in which she describes her life.

"He Leadeth Me"

When life is darkest, then ofttimes I feel
His hand clasps mine in tenderness and love,
And though I cannot see the way, I know full well
He will not let me fall, and so
I clasp more tightly the dear hand
That leads me onward, onward to my quiet rest.

Thanks, dear ones for every kindly word,
Affection ever sends her cheerful rays
Down, deep down into the imprisoned soul.
And though all is dark around her silent chambers
Are full of light, with sympathy and love,
Our father leads us all, but most
He pities his poor sightless child!

Cynthia was born on the summit of one of the highest hills in Berkshire, Massachusetts, on February 27, 1826. Her family was poor and lived in a

Cynthia Millicent Roberts Gorton, also known as Ida Glenwood, the Blind Bard of Michigan. *Fenton Historical Society.*

humble home, but their deep religious beliefs made them appreciate what little they had. Her father, Samuel Roberts, died when Cynthia was one year old. Her mother did her best to care for her five children.

As a child, Cynthia was known as foolish and rosy-cheeked, and she was always making rhymes. Elders did not appreciate her silliness, so she kept to herself. Known as a deep thinker, she wondered about the mysteries of life and death and enjoyed the grandeur of nature.

Cynthia continued to live with her widowed mother while she attended the seminary of Madame Willard in Troy, New York. It was around this time that she began seeing shadows within her eyes. She liked school and enjoyed writing compositions in a style that caught the attention of many of her instructors. Cynthia's mother passed away, leaving her an orphan at the age of fourteen. The combination of the tears she shed over her loss of her dear mother and her application to study produced an inflammation in Cynthia's eyes. When Cynthia was unable to resume her studies, her teacher Mrs. Willard hoped she could stay on as a teacher scholar, but her limited eyesight made the opportunity an impossibility.

At the age of twenty-one, Cynthia married Frederick Gorton, a prosperous paper manufacturer. Six years later, she endured a painful and lingering illness in which a curtain of darkness covered her eyes, and she became blind. Once her physical strength returned after the three-year illness, Cynthia began to write, but she had to depend on a scribe, which limited her ability to create what her heart wished to express.

The couple moved from New York in the early 1870s and made Fenton their home. They lived at 108 South Pine Street. Cynthia continued to write—that is, with an assistant. Frederick became an insurance agent, realtor, and machinery broker. Their adopted daughter, Ida Glenwood Gorton, was the first woman insurance agent in Fenton and worked alongside her father.

"The Fatal Secret" was Cynthia's first work of prose, and it was written in pencil. She had written it so quickly, it was nearly unreadable and looked to form a new alphabet. Her life changed to one of subtle independence when she acquired one of the first manufactured typewriters. She was proficient in pressing the keys, seldom making a mistake. Not only did she write poems, but Cynthia also published two books and submitted serial stories and poems to the *Detroit Christian Herald*, along with other papers and periodicals.

The "Blind Bard of Michigan," or, as she was also known, the "Sweet Singer," performed many of her poems, reciting them from memory. Her oratorical ability impressed many when she recited a particularly long poem for an hour and a half. Even Governor Reuben Fenton of New York said, "One must conclude, after listening to the Blind Bard of Michigan, that if we would find the best and deepest poetical thoughts, we must look for them in the emanations from the imprisoned soul." Cynthia lectured before large audiences for twenty years before settling in a quieter lifestyle due to exhaustion.

Cynthia became a member of the Shut-in Band and sent words of comfort and sympathy to lonely hearts. Being of a conservative religious nature, she also recited her poems at temperance gatherings.

The Blind Bard of Michigan took her last breath at 3:00 p.m. on August 5, 1894, leaving behind her beloved husband, who was buried next to her in section G of Oakwood Cemetery in October 1905, and her dear daughter, Ida Case.

Some of her works include *Fatal Secret*, 1873; *The Wife's Appear*, 1873; *Lily Pearl and the Mistress of Rosedale*, 1892; and many others. The following is another poem she wrote.

"Alone All Night"

Hark! What's that?—a sound I hear!
Someone is at the door, I fear!
There! O, no—'twas not a step;
The wind perhaps! I must have slept!
O—it is dreary, one must own
To stay all night in the house alone!

This darkness wraps me like a pall!
Rearing around my bed a wall
So high, the air seems damp and chill!
And I, imprisoned, mind and will!
O—it is dreary, one must own,
To stay all night in the house alone!

Is all the world asleep or dead?
It seems so still around my bed.
And yet if a slight noise I hear,
I start as if a ghost was near!
O—it is dreary, one must own,
To stay all night in the house alone!

Ah—there's a clock! It's only one!
The midnight hour has but just gone!
When will the sluggard, laggard night
Draw back her curtains from the light?
O—it is dreary, one must own,
To stay all night in the house alone!

"Tick, tick," the busy clock works on,
Time drags the heavy hours along!
And morning always with her light
Has followed close the darkness night.
Yet it is dreary one must own,
To stay all night in the house alone!

The Fenton Grain Elevator

In 1865, J.R. Mason built the Fenton Grain Elevator opposite the Vermont House, now known as the Fenton Hotel. This wood-framed building has clapboard, also known as board and batting, siding. Rectangular in shape, it stands between two and three and a half stories tall with irregular rooflines and is adjacent to the railroad tracks running through Fenton. Two years later, Mason sold it to D.G. Colwell and E.M. Adams. In the 1880s, it handled about 20 percent of all the wheat produced in Genesee County.

Grain elevators were of vital importance to not only Fenton but other communities as well. They were gathering points for farmers in the surrounding area, where they visited, exchanged ideas, and devised solutions for farming and livestock problems. Grain elevators were usually found along the railroad system about every six to ten miles, giving farmers only a short distance to travel with their loaded horse-drawn wagons and, later, their trucks. The wagons or trucks would pull into the unloading docks, where they would be weighed. The farmers would unload their grain through an opening in the floor, and then the vehicles would be weighed again. A sample of the grain would be taken. Based on the weight and quality of the grain, the farmers would receive payment. Below ground level, the grain would be scooped into small containers, or half-buckets, on a vertical belt and sorted into a holding bin. The grain would later be disbursed into a railroad car for shipping or put into burlap bags to be purchased by the residents in the area. The rail system often had several branches, with one beside the grain elevator.

The Fenton Grain Elevator changed ownership again in the 1880s to Mr. Stoner and Mr. Smith.

In 1883, Burdick Potter operated in no. 2 of the Andrews block on the southwest corner of Leroy Street and West Shiawassee Avenue. His residence was located at 305 Rockwell Street. He was a dealer and manufacturer of harness whips, horse clothing, and trunks and a wholesaler of county produce. He owned an elevator on the west side of North Leroy Street, just north of the railroad tracks. By 1885, Potter's produce business had increased to the point that he needed additional storage. He purchased the Fenton Grain Elevator from Stoner and Smith and began stocking it with corn, oats, flour, feed, lime, salt, and other items. He removed his stock of harness and whips to his produce elevator and sold the items at a discount. Potter was known as a reliable buyer of produce and always paid a fair price to the farmers. He purchased apples by the barrels. At one time, he purchased 1,700 barrels, which he shipped, and he still had 1,200 barrels of apples in storage. He was particularly fond of beans. To put a pinch on his competition, he painted "Me want beans too" on his elevator window. His advertising worked. He had loads of beans brought in by farmers near and far. In 1886, he had over 4,000 bushels of beans. He traveled to Washington,

The Burdick Potter Coal and Wood Yard in the grain elevator. *Fenton Historical Society*.

D.C., to negotiate for the sale of his beans with President Cleveland and other parties. He began a Fenton building boom later that year when he added a twenty-by-one-hundred-foot warehouse that included two stories and a cellar.

Like most grain elevators, the railroad system was of vital importance to farmers, as it allowed for the shipment of the grain. The railroad tracks in Fenton traveled between the two depots, the north depot for cargo and the south depot for passengers, and continued northwest, past the two grain elevators. It branched off to unload coal at two large storage sheds. The tracks extended west toward the train's next destination.

In 1980, the Fenton Grain Elevator was added to the National Register of Historic Places. At one time, the Fenton Grain Elevator housed antique shops. The last to inhabit the building was an outfitter retailer.

During one of the grain elevator's renovations, workers experienced doors slamming, sudden cold drafts and strange sounds echoing throughout various sections of the building.

CHARLES "LEFT HAND CHARLIE" ANDREW DAMON

Charles Andrew Damon was an actor, sharpshooter, gun collector, salesman, landlord, and fruit grower. To the citizens of Fenton, he was affectionally known as "Charlie." He was instrumental in collecting photographs for the 1934 Fenton centennial by rescuing many of the photographs from trash barrels, fires, and long-forgotten dusty trunks stored in attics. His collection makes up a large portion of the records of the Fenton Historical Society that are kept in the A.J. Phillips Fenton Museum.

Charlie was born on July 3, 1863, in Parma, Monroe County, New York. His father, George E. Damon, moved his family to Fenton and operated a grocery business on the south side of the Shiawassee River. It was located at 409 South Leroy Street. The family lived on the second floor of the building.

At a young age, Charlie became proficient with a firearm. He would shoot off the jug handles of vinegar jars and aim at eggs tossed into the air. He could have worked in his father's grocery store, but he was drawn to a different career. In his twenties, he became a member of a traveling theatrical group. On August 9, 1886, he performed at the Colwell Opera House of Fenton in Wallace's Standard Dramatic Company's five-act drama, *The Octoroon*. He also played in *The Miner's Daughter*. Charlie's marksmanship, both with a pistol and rifle, was featured during many traveling shows. His demonstrations included shooting an apple off the head of his assistant, cutting cards, and hitting coins. Since he was left-handed, Charlie was known as "Left Hand Charlie, celebrated scout and Indian fighter." Posters and advertisements proclaimed he was the only left-handed snap rifle and pistol shot in America, shooting a rifle in over fifty different positions, and performing over fifty tricks with pistols and six-shooters. At Fenton's annual fair in August 1888, Charlie demonstrated his shooting skills. He shot the ashes off a lit cigar that was held in the mouth of his assistant and shot clay disks that were tossed into the air. In October that year, he exhibited his shooting skills with the Bronco John Company, based out of Cincinnati, Ohio. The Detroit International Exposition, a precursor to the Michigan State Fair, engaged Left Hand Charlie to display his skills. He did so eloquently by shooting a glass ball from the helmeted head of his assistant. He performed at the Montreal exposition in 1892, which was held to celebrate the city's 250th anniversary.

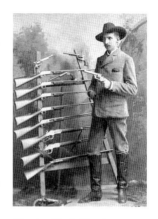

Charles "Left-Hand Charlie" Damon. *Fenton Historical Society.*

In between his exhibitions, Charlie operated shooting galleries in Bay City, Detroit and London, Ontario. He also penned a book titled *The Art of Shooting*. It was typeset, letter by letter, by the *Fenton Independent* newspaper. He explained his writing as follows:

> *I will try to put my ideas before you, just as if you had never fired a gun and came to me for a course of instruction, the same as you would do to become a musician or to learn some other art when the eye and hand must be trained to act in unison.*

He also advised his readers:

> *Do not murder innocent birds or animals merely to gratify your taste for blood, or a cruel desire to take life. There are plenty of vermin and birds of prey to practice on. Never kill more game than you can use or kill game while it is sitting. It is more sportsmanlike to kill game while flying or running, give the game an equal chance of life, besides showing the ingenuity and skill over the powers of self-preservation, which nature has provided all living things. In handling firearms, great care must be exercised to guard against any accident either to yourself or anyone else.*

Always handle any firearm as if it were loaded, and never allow a gun to be pointed toward anyone.

Charlie represented several gun manufacturers and traveled the world. His vast gun collection, containing over four hundred firearms, was described as one of the finest and unique in the Midwest. He lived in the lovely house facing Freedom Park, once the town square, at 308 West Shiawassee Avenue, built in 1878 as part of Phillips Row.

Charles Andrew Damon. *Fenton Historical Society.*

After the Fenton centennial in 1934, Charlie's health began to fail. He sold his gun collection and moved his family to a smaller house on South East Street. He passed away on September 29, 1937, at the age of seventy-four. He was buried in Oakwood Cemetery in section D.

HORTON-COLWELL OPERA HOUSE

As the budding downtown of Fenton continued to evolve, Dexter Horton and David Colwell built a place for gathering and the performing arts at the southeast corner of South Leroy and Caroline Streets in 1869. It was known as the Horton-Colwell Opera House. However, the name was shortened to Colwell Opera House for ease of reference. It was dedicated on February 1, 1870. Its brickwork is embellished with the letters "FLT," a symbol of the Independent Order of the Odd Fellows fraternal organization. FLT is an abbreviation for their motto, "Friendship, love and truth."

The Colwell Opera House was more than a place to watch performances; it also housed a general store, and U.S. post office from 1869 to 1883 on the first floor. The opera house was located on the second floor, which was divided into two rooms: a waiting room and the performance room. Organizations, such as schools, churches, and fraternal and other clubs, used the opera house for their gatherings and performances. Admission was usually twenty-five cents for adults and fifteen cents for children. In 1879, General Tom Thumb, part of P.T. Barnum's circus, performed to the thrill of those in attendance. The Fenton Ladies' Band rented the opera house and played on stage in 1883 while people paid ten cents to roller skate. The skate rental cost five cents. The building was also used for the annual Knights Templar's Ball, school plays, graduations, and shows by performers who were traveling to Fenton by train. Tom Thumb's performance of *Uncle Tom's Cabin* was particularly popular. Edison's first motion picture, *Monkeyshines, No. 1*, was viewed by many in the opera house. Reserved seats cost twenty cents, and general admission cost fifteen cents for an individual and seventy-five cents for a family. *Monkeyshines, No. 1* was created between June 1889 and November 1890 by William Dickson, an engineer and employee of Edison who was in charge of the project. The invention used to view a motion picture was called a Kinetoscope. It was a large box that quickly moved a strip of film over a light source. Observers watched the motion picture from a hole in the top of the box. The rapidly moving film gave the impression of movement, much like a flipbook.

Charles A. Damon purchased the opera house in 1900 and sold it to Mrs. W.P. Cook in 1910. In the spring of 1910, panic rippled through the Fenton community as rumors spread that the end of the world was possible when Halley's Comet passed by Earth. Religious groups urged everyone to repent or be damned, and news reporters, with their exaggerated stories of poisonous gas in the comet's tail, seemed to rile people even more. It seemed as if the citizens of Fenton either accepted their impending doom or ignored the nonsense. Many purchased telescopes to ensure they obtained the perfect view of the comet. On the night Halley's Comet passed, families and friends gathered on their lawns. Others gathered in the Waterworks Park, now Millpond Park, or on street corners. For those who wanted a closer view, they stood on the rooftop of the Colwell Opera House with a complimentary drink in their hand. All eyes searched the stary sky. As Halley's Comet was spotted, everyone cheered and then stared in awe at the large, white, glowing ball, with its long tail, as it traversed the sky.

The last owner of the Colwell Opera House was Frank Granger. He also owned a hardware store and was the mayor of Fenton. When he passed away, he bequeathed the building to his daughter Mrs. Frank Vaclavik of Holland, Michigan. The opera house was used as a roller-skating rink in the 1930s, until the floor was condemned. The building was last used as a dime store in 1975. When urban renewal descended on Fenton in 1978, the Colwall Opera House was dismantled and rebuilt on a smaller scale at Crossroads Village, north of Flint, using many of the harvested original bricks, ceiling beams, and casement windows. The reconstructed opera house was completed in 1980.

Many who own and operate old opera houses and theaters are aware of the lingering spirits of former actors and actresses. Employees of Crossroads Village claim the Colwell Opera House has active spirits who made the move from Fenton to the opera house's new location. They claim to see shadow figures darting around corners. The fragrance of lilacs often lingers heavily in the air. A disembodied female voice is often heard. Perhaps it is a past actress. Technical issues with the lighting occur regularly. Do you dare to step into the Colwell Opera House at Crossroads Village to view a performance?

THE FIRST PRESBYTERIAN CHURCH

On February 28, 1840, the First Presbyterian Church was organized in Fentonville. It had seventeen members and met in a three-story building on the northwest corner of West Shiawassee Avenue and South Leroy Street.

The first church was built in 1848 at the corner of Adelaide and Rockwell Streets. It was made of brick and burned in 1861.

In 1862, David L. LaTourette signed a deed to the lot where the church is today on March 7, and Elizabeth Birdsall provided an additional half lot on May 1 that year. The Board of Church Erection obtained a loan of $500. A year later, the wooden building of the Presbyterian church was built using one-inch-thick boards that were twelve inches wide, and strips of battens covered the cracks between the boards.

A lot on the southeast corner of Leroy and Rockwell Streets was purchased in 1891. The money used to obtain the property was raised by the ladies of the church, who supplemented a $1,500 loan by making and serving meals and desserts on the fairgrounds during Fenton's Fall Fair. The Fenton Fairgrounds were located east of Hickory Street, now Lemen Street, and north of South Street, now South Holly Road.

Additions made to the church in 1899 included two alcoves and a choir loft, and the exterior was veneered with paving bricks.

One of the most sorrowful losses of the Fenton community occurred on March 7, 1911. Miss Rena Conrad, age eighteen and a member of the junior class of Fenton High School, succumbed to her yearlong illness of

First Presbyterian Church. *Brenda Hasse*.

rheumatism, which affected her heart. She was the daughter of Mr. and Mrs. Jay Conrad. Mr. Conrad, who owned Conrad's Café, was on the edge of death from neuralgia of the heart before the family secured a specialist from Detroit. Rena, in her excited and worried condition over her father's health, was removed from her house to the residence of L.M. Cook, a neighbor and druggist, where she took her last breath. Rena was an active member of the Young People's Society of the Presbyterian church and a leader of the younger social set of Fenton. Her death was said to cast a gloom over the students. Her funeral was scheduled to be conducted at her home, but with her father's fragile condition, the funeral was held at the First Presbyterian Church, with Reverend A.G. Work delivering the service. The church was decorated with floral offerings, the finest ever seen. One bouquet contained nine lilies, each representing Rena's closest friends, and one broken lily, representing Rena. The sorrowful bouquet attracted a lot of the mourners' attention. Rena's casket was carried by six of her male classmates. The mass was concluded with everyone singing "Beautiful Isle of Somewhere," and Rena's remains were buried in Oakwood Cemetery.

Two prominent sisters, Mrs. Elmira Bussey and Mrs. Mary A. Rackham, were instrumental in overseeing updates to the First Presbyterian Church in 1930 in honor of their mother, Mrs. Lavina Horton. They are credited with remodeling the parlors, the dining room, and the kitchen and installing a new heating system. In 1935, the congregation voted to purchase a new organ and much-needed carpet. Mrs. Bussey stepped forward and saw the impossible task completed through her donation. Occasionally, a single key on the organ will play by itself. Some say it is the ghost of Mrs. Bussey reminding everyone that nothing is impossible and that she is nearby and still watching over the church.

THE EDWIN TRUMP AND GEORGE WASHINGTON WILMOT HOUSES

During a time when banks were privately owned and the owners could not always be trusted, long before the FDIC ensured deposits, several banks in Fentonville folded, and depositors lost their savings. The Trump and Wilmot Bank was one such institution. The bank was owned by partners Edwin Trump and George Washington Wilmot. They nearly broke their bank over a silly competition to see who could build the most magnificent house in town.

It was 1867 when the challenge between the partners was made. Wilmot's house at 501 South East Street is a big white Italian villa–style home that also has some Gothic ornamentation. It is located on the southeast corner of East and Rockwell Streets. Trump's Gothic revival house is located at 801 South East Street, on the southeast corner of East and High Streets. The third floor of Trump's house has ceilings so high that it contained a trapeze and basketball hoop to entertain the young residents. Boy scout meetings were held there, too.

The collapse of the Trump and Wilmot Bank began when a wealthy

The George Washington Wilmot house. *Brenda Hasse.*

German farmer by the name of Robert Holtforth was impressed by Wilmot's house. Holtforth decided he wanted to build big, beautiful houses, too. He withdrew all his money from the bank. Once word got out, people panicked. Everyone withdrew their money from the bank, causing its collapse.

In 1872, Trump traded his house to A.U. Wood, a local attorney, for a business block in downtown Fenton.

Mr. Eddy's Trolley

George Marion Eddy was born in Erie County, Pennsylvania, on November 5, 1834. His father, Nathan Eddy, a farmer, brought his family to Fenton Township on the outskirts of Fentonville in Genesee County in 1841. George was seven years old and attended school on slab seats in a rustic log cabin. When he reached the age of eighteen, his father allowed him to choose his own career. George decided to learn carpentry. So, he did. After saving his earned pay, in 1855, he purchased 160 acres of land northeast of Fentonville. The land was thought to be untamable, but George set to work, organized it, and made it a productive farm.

George married Jane McOmber, whose parents were some of the first settlers in the state of Michigan. Jane passed away in 1890, leaving behind three children: Hattie Eddy Cook, who married Leslie Cook, a prominent pharmacist; Charles S., a successful businessman and the owner of the finest livery in Fenton; and Marion E., a farmer. George was remarried on January 21, 1891, to Hattie Wells.

George was a staunch Republican and identified strongly with the Knights Templar. On his expansive farm, in 1885, he purchased a magnificent horse, Golden King, described as a fine specimen of the Hambletonian family, and began raising trotting horses. His horses, with their superior lineage, were sold throughout New England.

Charles owned a livery, the largest in town, with twelve horses. It was located approximately at 327 North Leroy Street. He rented his horses to

Eddy and his sons. *Fenton Historical Society.*

traveling salesmen, or, as they were known then, "drummers." An aggressive businessman, Charles always had a coach waiting at the depot to meet the train of travelers and convey them to their desired destination. His horses also helped transport the hook and ladder fire department's equipment and men when necessary. One day, one of his coach drivers pulled up to the depot to meet the arriving passengers of the train. The driver dismounted, leaving the coach unattended. As a guest entered the coach, in need of transportation, the bell rang to alert the fire department of a fire. On cue, the horses darted toward the fire station, anticipating their duty to transport the equipment and men to the fire. The startled passenger held on for dear life, not knowing his destination in the driverless coach.

In 1887, George purchased steamer boats and added them to his property that he owned on Long Lake, now Lake Fenton. In 1889, he purchased an abandon car line or trolley system from Muskegon and brought it to Fenton. The horse-drawn cars on the narrow-gauge rail system ran from the Fenton Hotel to Long Lake, where he also had a small waterfront resort with a wraparound porch. After receiving donations for its expense in 1891, George enlisted the support of volunteers to grade the roadbed and lay the track. By July, Genesee County's first streetcar was in full operation. His horse-drawn trollies would take guests to and from the resort twice a day

City of Fenton steamboat, the smaller *Maccabee* steamboat (*left*), and campers in the background on Long Lake. *Fenton Historical Society*.

Eddy's cottage and trolley. *Fenton Historical Society*.

The *City of Fenton* on Long Lake. *Fenton Historical Society.*

during the summer months. When attendance increased for a holiday or picnic events, it was necessary to have the trolley pulled by two horses. There were times, however, when the over-loaded trolley needed a push from passengers, as a single horse would labor up the grade from the lake. One of the horses that pulled the trolley was blind. The driver often bragged how it never stumbled, while other horses often stumbled on the plank road. The driver of each trolley earned twenty-five cents a day, making the round trip from the depot to Eddy's Landing twice a day. After working their way up, a driver could become a conductor and receive an increase in pay to thirty-five cents per day. The top job belonged to the barn boss, who received five dollars per week.

In 1894, George and his sons purchased a large boat called the *City of Fenton*. It was ninety-two feet long from bow to stern and sixteen feet wide. It was a double-decker steamer ship that held a capacity of over six hundred people. George employed the Fenton Ladies' Band to perform concerts on the steamer and encouraged guests to enjoy a cruise around the lake while listening to the music. George decided to give up his lake business in 1903. The *City of Fenton* was pulled up to the south side of the shore. Eventually, it was taken apart piece by piece.

George sold the trolley business to George Bridson, who operated it for several years until 1916, when he dismantled the tracks.

LIVERIES

In the early years of Fenton, horses and buggies were the main mode of transportation. Even though many households had a carriage house, few had the space to accommodate a horse. Several liveries in town offered their fine horses for rent. The proprietors of the liveries owned several horses that they would rotate, and they would limit each horse to the number of days per week it would work. Some of the horses were farm horses that were used to plow fields, while others were rented for pulling buggies or riding. Some were standing ready to respond to the church bell, which indicated the need for the hook and ladder firemen to put out a fire. There were five liveries in town, along with a ten-cent barn.

At the corner of Roberts (now Silver Lake Road) and River Streets was the ten-cent barn, now the State Bank, owned by Mrs. L.G. Peers. It was not a livery stable. When people on the outskirts of town arrived with their horse, they could leave it at the barn for ten cents; it would be fed and watered. The owner of the horse had to provide their own oats. To convey to the owner of the animal that it would be well cared for, the barn was kept spotless and clean—not a cobweb in sight.

Dapper men and their horse. *Fenton Historical Society.*

George Marion Eddy and his sons owned the largest livery, with one dozen horses. It was located on North Leroy Street at approximately 327 North Leroy Street, where Fenton Glass is today.

Just a few buildings south from Eddy's livery was another stable, which was located directly across the street from the Fenton Hotel. It is assumed many of the hotel's guests may have rented a horse and/or horse and buggy from that stable or from Eddy.

At 115 West Shiawassee Avenue was the Hotel Livery. With hotels at the corner of West Shiawassee Avenue and Leroy Street, this livery not only rented out its horses, but it also most likely housed a few horses for hotel guests while they stayed in town.

Alan Gunning's barn was located on the northeast corner of Ellen and East Streets. Gunning was a trainer of pacers, or trotter racehorses, but he traded horses, too. He had a few horses for hire.

Livery owners from other towns would report when an exhausted horse was ridden too hard. It was the neighborly thing to do and ensured all the livery horses were treated kindly. It was a policy of livery owners to refuse renting any of their horses to abusive offenders.

Around 1900, Mr. Van Atta arrived from Detroit and opened a livery at 112 Roberts Street. Today, its location would have been in the parking lot of the Horizon building at 102 Silver Lake Road. Van Atta had four horses for hire and two other horses that many knew by the names of Fat Dan and Slim Dan. Van Atta sold his livery to Mr. Butcher. Shortly after Butcher took ownership, a fire broke out in the barn. Of the five horses, only Slim Dan was saved. It was rumored the charred bones of the deceased horses were paved over when a car wash was built on the property. In all likelihood, they may still be there today.

The Underground Railroad

The Underground Railroad began in the 1830s. Fleeing slaves could hear shouting men and barking dogs as they ran through fields, dodged trees in thick woods, and waded through swamps in the hopes of losing their pursers. Bounty hunters were always a problem. Many of the escaped slaves were hunted down, captured, and usually severely punished. The lucky ones were never caught.

The Civil War was a trying time for the United States. Many believe slavery was the main cause for the war between the North and the South, but that is only partially true. The secession of the South was a result of the decision to make recently acquired land west of the Mississippi River free of slavery. President Abraham Lincoln did not want to take the enslaved away from the South, because he knew they were vital to the region's economy. But once the South seceded, Lincoln was determined to keep the country united and wrote the Emancipation Proclamation. The proclamation did not free the enslaved population but gave Union soldiers the authority to confiscate enslaved people in the South, bring them northward and set them free. Unfortunately, bounty hunters waited to snatch freed slaves and collect their due reward.

Risking their lives for freedom, escapees traveled at night, using the stars as guides. They were referred to as "cargo" or "fares" in search of a "conductor" or "stationmaster" who was empathetic to their plight. Safehouses were dotted along the way, approximately fifteen miles apart, as escapees traveled northward along the line. They searched for a house or barn that may have had a quilt displayed in an attic window, a star on a wall or gable or a lit lantern of a jockey statue in front of the house, indicating it was a place where escapees could rest their heads during the day before traveling along the next leg of their journey. Sometimes, a conductor would take the cargo and either led them by foot or transport them in the back of a wagon beneath a stack of hay to the next stop to ensure they arrived safely. However, to keep the line a secret, the conductor only knew the next stop. If he was ever questioned by the authorities, he could not provide the number of stops along the route, their locations or where the line originated in Kentucky or Missouri. Occasionally, a worker on a train would allow an escaped slave to ride in a boxcar. Coded messages would appear in local newspapers to alert stationmasters of an arriving escapee. A coded message may have read, "light brown fillies and brown and tan pups," which meant young girls and several mixed-race children would be arriving. Anyone involved with harboring an escaped slave was putting their life at risk, but conductors were willing to take that chance.

Several routes northward led to a main crossing point from Michigan to Windsor, Canada. Detroit was the destination for most enslaved people. However, when a bounty hunter or the authorities were a roadblock to the cargo's freedom, the conductor diverted the "train" to an alternative route. One of those alternatives went through the village of Fentonville. Two households were known to offer a safe place for escapees to rest before departing for the next station.

SINCLAIR STREET

This historic home was built in 1840, possible by David L. LaTourette, who owned a bank and donated properties and funding to the construction of buildings within Fentonville. This house was once declared the sturdiest home in Fenton due to its double-rowed brick walls and its basement made of concrete poured over heavy stone walls. It was on route no. 6 of the Underground Railroad system. The house is located on a quiet street adjacent to the Oakwood Cemetery. Fleeing slaves knew this house was a station, a safe stop to rest or hide. On the LaTourette farm, there was a barn in which escapees could hide. LaTourette would instruct his family to not go in the barn when he expected cargo. The enslaved would be on their way early the next morning.

Henry Riggs House

Another stop on the Underground Railroad was the Henry Riggs house, located at 207 West Shiawassee Avenue. There was a secret room beneath the dining room where escapees could hide. Escaped slaves could enter the room through a small door in the carriage house. In fear of being caught by the authorities, after a short rest and meal, they would leave. They did not want to cause trouble for the conductor or get caught by the authorities.

To Freedom

Once leaving Fenton, escapees headed toward Port Huron and crossed the Saint Clair River into Sarnia, Canada. After their weary feet touched the new land, many rejoiced. For the first time in their lives, they tasted freedom and celebrated in song.

CHARLES W. COE

Charles W. Coe was born in Connecticut in 1819. He was the youngest of three sons. As a young man, he went to New York City, where he learned the trade of blacksmithing. Coe left New York and settled in Ingham County, where he purchased 1,100 acres and opened a dry goods business. It was a life lesson indeed, as the business failed. He then married Ann. His daughter Mary was born on January 13, 1844, in Ashtabula County, Ohio. Coe moved his family to Corunna, Michigan, purchased a lot and built a store and residence. On November 7, 1861, at the age of forty-three, Coe enlisted in the Michigan First Cavalry Battalion, Company H. His daughter Mary wed James E. Bussey on December 31 that same year. Coe had the honor of serving under Brigadier General George Armstrong Custer at the Battle of Gettysburg. He saw many men fall during the ten battles in which he fought. He returned home at the end of the war and resumed working in his business. Shortly afterward, a fire destroyed his business and residence. He sold the lot and moved to Fentonville, where he returned to his trade of blacksmithing and built a home at 308 South Holly Road. Coe invented the first power drill, which was operated by hand, and improved it over time. It was sold throughout the United States and exported to Prussia, Russia, and England. Others tried to infringe on his patents. His case was finally tried by the Supreme Court of the United States, which ruled in his favor. Coe built the C.W. Coe Drilling Manufactory on the southeast corner of East Shiawassee Avenue and Oak Street. The plant manufactured drills, twist drills, tire-up-setters, and tire binders. Coe passed away in his home on July 16, 1888. James, his son-in-law, took over the running of his factory and ran a hardware store in town as well. Coe's granddaughter's husband Wallace Gurnea became the manager of the factory but passed away two years later, leaving behind his wife, Grace.

Coe was a member of the Episcopal church and was one of the oldest members of the Fenton Commandery of the Knights Templar and the Sovereign Consistory of Detroit. He and his wife were buried in section E of Oakwood Cemetery.

A NUTRITION-CONSCIOUS GHOST

Located on Silver Lake Road is a retail store that offers natural remedies, supplements, essential oils, crystals, and other items that are used to lift everyone's spirits and help customers achieve optimal health. Not only are the employees courteous and helpful, but the energy within the store has a positive vibe. However, there seems to be more than the products, customers, and employees within its walls. Some believe the strange happenings experienced by the employees are the results of a friendly ghost or angels overseeing their work.

While alone in the store, an employee was busy at the front counter, pricing items and adding them to the inventory. She kept hearing the crinkling of chip bags and the rustling of items on a shelf. Believing someone had entered the store without her noticing, she went to the aisle to offer her assistance but found no one there. She searched the store, but other than the manager, who was in her office, she was alone. This has also happened to other employees on several occasions.

On another occasion, one of the employees went to ask her two coworkers behind the counter a question. As she began to speak, the two employees froze and stared as a translucent person in a white, wispy gown walked behind the questioning employee. The translucent apparition quickly vanished. The two women looked at each other as if silently asking whether they had both seen the same thing. It was confirmed they had indeed, and they relayed the information to the third employee.

Could a health-conscious spirit be pleased by the assistance and advice the employees give to their customers? Whatever the intention of this spirit may be, it appears to be friendly.

DOCTOR ISAAC WIXOM

Isaac Wixom was born the third son of ten children in Hector, Schuyler County, New York, on March 7, 1803. He attended a common school until the age of seventeen. His mother passed away in 1816. He then attended Geneva Academy in Geneva, New York. After attending the academy for two years, he focused on his study of medicine in the office of the county physician. During his stay at the academy, his father's business failed, and he could no longer pay for Isaac's education. Isaac took it upon himself to teach classes and earn the money necessary to complete his education. Surpassing his instructors' knowledge, he attended and studied medicine at Fairfield, Herkimer County, New York, and graduated, but because of his minority, was not given a diploma. When Isaac was twenty-one, he received a medical diploma from Penn Yan in Yates County. On March 18, 1824, he married Maria Ryal. For four years, Isaac practiced medicine in Steuben County, New York. In the spring of 1829, he relocated to Farmington, Michigan, and returned to New York in the autumn to collect his family and take them to their new home. He was elected justice of the peace of Farmington Township in 1837. In 1838, he was elected as a representative to the legislature for Oakland County, which met in Detroit. For two years, he was a member of the House Committee on Education, taking an active part in the founding of the University of Michigan and other educational institutions. He declined a renomination to the house in 1841 and was elected to the senate for the Sixth District in 1842. Doctor Wixom was the chairman on the Committee on Claims. He also drew up the first railroad charter in the state. Isaac retired from politics in 1843 and devoted himself to his medical practice. By 1845, he had the largest medical and surgical practice in the state. Doctor Wixom moved his family to Argentine, Genesee County, and platted the village the following year. He operated a grocery store, a gristmill, and an acclaimed hotel that was the finest in Genesee County, and he donated land for a nonsectarian church. In June 1845, he became nationally known for performing the first hip joint amputation, separating the socket and ball, and arresting the case of tuberculosis of the bone.

At the start of the Civil War, in 1861, Isaac helped Colonel Thomas Stockton to recruit men for the Stockton Independent Regiment, later known as the Sixteenth Michigan Infantry. Doctor Wixom was the infantry's surgeon and followed them through twenty-two battles, performing a second hip joint amputation in December 1862. After two years, Doctor Wixom had to resign due to his failing health. He returned home to his medical practice. In 1870, he moved to Fenton and built a house at 714 West Shiawassee Avenue that was described as having a cupola.

Doctor Wixom was a Freemason at the age of twenty-one and took all the degrees offered in the United States. He educated forty men in medicine and surgery, many of whom became renowned doctors. One of his sons, William Wallace Wixom, was a noted surgeon in the state of California. Doctor Wixom had a total of six children. He was described as a courteous and a conversational man. He gave freely to those who deserved it, aiding others without a thought to his income. He continued to practice medicine, teach others, and perform surgery into his seventies. Doctor Isaac Wixom died on July 24, 1880, and he was buried in Oakwood Cemetery in Fenton.

THE OBSCURE AND DIFFERENT

Every town has them—the people who are avoided by most. These undesirables receive sidewise glances, stares and whispered comments that are just out of their earshot. They notice others' inquisitive glances. When they return the strangers' piercing stares, the guilty turn away as if they were caught being judgmental. Many of those who are different are born into uncontrollable circumstances that cause people to assume the worst. Whatever the reason, most citizens sidestepped to avoid the following trio of Fenton citizens.

THE BUZZARD BROTHERS

As citizens walked along the sidewalk or shopped in the stores along Leroy Street, they glanced in the direction of the sound of a tractor engine echoing in the distance. Tractors belong on a farm, not on the main street of town. As the sound grew nearer, they stopped and stared in disbelief at the sight of the Buzzard brothers driving their tractor down Leroy Street.

Their father, Israel Buzzard, served in the Civil War. A legendary tale says a fellow soldier announced to the family that Israel was on his way home. The children waited at the end of the driveway to see him as soon as he crested sandy Denton Hill toward home. Dressed in his travel-stained blue uniform, his Springfield rifle on his shoulder, the children alerted their mother that their father was home.

The family was quite poor, uneducated, uncultured, and uncouth. Furthermore, they seldom bathed. One kind neighbor always wrapped the leftovers of their holiday meals and sent them to the Buzzard family to enjoy. It was the Christian thing to do.

THE OLD TIMERS

When Herb Denton and Billy Thompson carried their drums into downtown Fenton, people cringed because they knew what would happen next. During the 1930s, the men, nicknamed the "old timers," would begin at one end of town and stand in front of a store. Herbert beat a slow beat on a bass drum, while Bill produced a rolling beat on his snare drum. They kept up the annoying racket until the storeowner could no longer stand the disruption. The storeowner would pay the two men a small sum or offer them a free meal. Then the men would move to the next store. The process would be repeated until they had stood before every store in town and reaped their reward. Those on the sidewalks would walk swiftly, cover their ears, and smile at their cleverness. The bass drum originally belonged to Bill. He had purchased it from a Civil War soldier. Herbert wanted the drum and purchased it from Bill, who was content to play the snare drum.

JOE SMALLBONE

On September 28, 1911, George and Phoebe Smallbone welcomed their son Joseph Milo into this world. His grandfather, Milo Crawford, was one of the town's early lamplighters before electricity was introduced in Fenton. The family of three lived on Wakeman Street. Joseph, or, as he was known, Joe, attended Fenton public schools. He lived with his mother until she passed away in 1947, leaving the house to Joe at the age of forty-four. He never married.

Joe was an eccentric individual. He never bathed, avoided eye contact, and often mumbled his replies. Some believe he may have had Asperger's Syndrome, which is defined as "a form of Autism Spectrum Disorder, is a developmental disorder. People with Asperger's Syndrome have difficulty relating to other people socially and their behavior and thinking pattern can be rigid and repetitive." When Joe visited a store to purchase supplies, the storeowners would spray their counters and the money he used with Lysol. People outside of Fenton knew him as the "Hermit of Fenton."

His house was easily recognizable. Joe had two Model A Fords, which he drove until they were inoperable and then remained parked in his yard. Afterward, he rode his old, dilapidated bicycle throughout town. His house was heated with a wood-burning stove, and his clothing, hands and face were always covered with soot. He was also a hoarder. When entering his house, a narrow pathway could be seen that led from room to room. Yet despite his way of living, Joe was a self-taught genius. He could fix electronics, and everyone in town would take their broken TVs and radios to Joe to fix. A man of little words, he always knew what was happening in town by talking to friends over the telephone.

Joe was an individual who was different, and the people of Fenton accepted him for who he was. They defended him when others would make mean comments, for they knew that behind the dirt and grime, his brown eyes conveyed kindness. They spoke highly of Joe and returned his kindness. The children treated him with respect, often visited him, and enjoyed watching him repair electronics.

Joe was never employed. Some people in town ensured he received Social Security. He was also paid for any repair he made to a TV or radio. Leo Weigant, Joe's friend and a former mayor of Fenton, was quoted as saying, "The Social Security, along with any money from small repairs, was his income."

One of Joe's longtime friends and Fenton social worker, Nancy Stockham, put together a box of food for his Christmas gift. It was so heavy the paperboy had to help her carry it. On that frigid Christmas Eve, Joe greeted them on the porch and proceeded to examine the label on every can. He did not like preservatives in his food. Even though they were quite cold, Stockham and the paperboy waited patiently for his approval. She said, "We were both freezing, exhausted and frustrated by the time we left."

One spring, Joe was using a hand plow when he cut his leg. The local druggist George Hovey treated his injury with a bag balm. Some believe Joe would have lost his leg had it not been for the druggist.

In 1881, Stockham took towels, soap, and clean clothes to Joe's house and helped him get ready for his fiftieth Fenton High School reunion at the Fenton Community Center. Stockham used her whit to coerce him into cleaning himself up for the event. She even teasingly stated that she was his date for the evening. Joe was clean and dapper; he went to his reunion and had a good time. His classmates gathered and posed for a class photograph. Joe stood in the back row, a few steps away from his classmates. It is one of only two known photographs ever taken of Joe Smallbone.

Weigant was quoted in 1996: "In society today, there is no room for eccentrics. Joe would have been hospitalized or institutionalized. I think, in Fenton, it was a mark of kindness that we let him suffer. He created a contented feeling in our lot. Joe Smallbone's life was a success. He, more than anyone I know, created a feeling of fulfillment in our town. We are richer because of his time here and poorer because of his going."

On January 9, 1885, Joseph Milo Smallbone died. His body was discovered in his yard a short distance from his house. He had frozen to death. He was buried in Oakwood Cemetery. It's easy to find his resting place—just look for the headstone in the shape of a Model A Ford. It respectfully reads, "A legend in his own time."

Additional Quotes of Remembrance

In July 1996, several people were interviewed and shared their opinions of Fenton's eccentric Joe Smallbone.

> *I was criticized because I didn't have Joe shown* [in an open casket], *but I felt if you didn't call on him when he was alive, there was no sense in gawking at him when he was dead.*
> —*Nancy Stockham, Fenton social worker*

> *I used to go up to Joe's with my dad and, later, by myself. The guys from the window factory were always taking radios and TVs that no one else would work on to Joe.*
> —*Jerry Palmer, Fenton fire chief*

> *Joe was a member of the Fenton High School class of 1931. He was odd but very smart, very good in math and science.*
> —*Dorothy Bush, former classmate*

> *He was a smart boy, real brainy. He was up on the sciences.*
> —*Ivar Strom, former classmate*

Shull Woodworth kept Joe in freshly caught fish. He used to clean them on newspapers on the back porch using an electric razor. It was a trip and a half to watch the process.
—Nancy Stockham, Fenton social worker

When we gave him wood or food, we felt kind. When we respected his privacy by not taking pictures, we felt good. When we showed visitors our local eccentric, we felt proud.
—Leo Weigant, former Fenton mayor and friend to Joe Smallbone

A Tribute to Joe Smallbone

Bonnie Whitehurst, a former Fenton resident and 1973 graduate of Fenton High School, is a musician, composer, music teacher, and recording artist. She created a song about Joe Smallbone. It captures her observation of the resident eccentric and describes his life. The music video also includes several photographs of Fenton and a picture of Joe's final resting place. You may find the video on youtube or on her website.

A Recent Sighting of Joe

A resident who lives across the street from Joe's former house claims his dogs will sometimes bark during the night. Upon looking out the window, he can see a man dressed in black crossing the street. Then the person disappears—simply vanishes. Perhaps Joe Smallbone is still among us.

BIBLIOGRAPHY

Books

American Biographical History of Eminent and Self-Made Men. Cincinnati, OH: Western Biographical Publishing Company, 1878.

Ellis, Franklin. "Banks: The First National Bank of Fenton." In *History of Genesee County Michigan. With Its Illustrations and Biographical Sketches of Its Prominent Men and Pioneers*. Philadelphia, PA: Everts and Abbott, 1879. Library of Congress. https://www.loc.gov/resource/gdcmassbookdig.historyofgenesee00elli/?sp=280&st=image.

————. "Colonel William Fenton." In *History of Genesee County Michigan. With Its Illustrations and Biographical Sketches of Its Prominent Men and Pioneers*. Philadelphia, PA: Everts and Abbott, 1879. https://www.loc.gov/resource/gdcmassbookdig.historyofgenesee00elli/?sp=220&st=image.

Hollister, Harvey J. "Banks and Bankers." In *The History of the City of Grand Rapids*. New York: Munsell and Company, 1891. Google Books. https://books.google.com/books?id=DWN5AAAAMAAJ&pg=PA667&source=gbs_toc_r&cad=4#v=onepage&q&f=false.

Peck, J.C. "Chapter XVI: By Horse Car to Long Lake." In *Local Lies, Legends, and Lore*. N.p.: self-published, November 1979.

Seger, Donna, and Kenneth Seger. *Postcard History Series, Fenton*. Charleston, South Carolina: Arcadia Publishing, 2009.

Silbar, Ruth Anne. *A Time to Remember, Fenton 1834 to Now.* De Pere, WI: Independent Printing Company Inc., 1976.

Wood, Edwin Orin. "The Lost Child." In *The History of Genesee County, Michigan: Her People, Industries and Institutions.* Indianapolis, IN: Federal Publishing Company, 1916.

ARTICLES

Burdick, Ray. "Memory Lane." *Fenton Independent*, n.d.

Fenton Historical Society Inc. "Hardware Store." Business and Professional History Project.

———. "Her Death Causes Gloom in Fenton." *Fenton Independent*, 1911.

———. "McHugh and McHugh Lumber Company." Business and Professional History Project.

———. "Park Club's First Meeting." *Fenton Independent*, December 1916.

———. "Pride in the Past; Confidence in the Future." Fenton Historical Site Tour, 1986.

———. "Reunion of 'Mystic Seven.'" *Fenton Independent*, September 14, 1910.

———. "Vintage Years for 'Ole Dobbin,' Fenton's Horse and Buggy Days Recalled." *Fenton Independent*, March 19, 1959.

Flint Journal. "Came to Fenton When That Section of Country Was a Wilderness—Funeral Held Today." February 27, 1907.

Hogan, V. "Historic Home Used During Underground Railroad Time." *Tri-County Times*, March 28, 1999.

———. "A Legend in His Own Time." *Tri-County Times*, October 16, 2015. https://www.tctimes.com/living/features/a-legend-in-his-own-time/article_885f6ba4-7443-11e5-bacb-83ea90072730.html.

———. "Local Train Depots Were Once Hubs of Activity." *Tri-County Times*, August 28, 2015. https://www.tctimes.com/living/local-train-depots-were-once-hubs-of-activity/article_93c35820-4dc4-11e5-9b3a-678b8f26e138.html.

———. "Tales of Eerie Hauntings as Told to Former Features Editor." *Tri-County Times*, October 25, 2019.

Michigan Gazeteer. "What Fentonville Was Like in 1856." 1856.

Rynearson, J. "Area Homeowners Detail Phenomena of Phantoms." *Fenton Independent*, October 29, 1980.

———. "Friendly Spirit Haunts F.A.R.R. Store." *Tri-County Times*, 1998.

———. "Haunted." *Tri-County Times*, October 27, 2002.

———. "Home Tour: Home Once Part of Underground Railway." *Tri-County Times*, 1989.

———. "In Search of the Flint-Genesee County Underground Railroad." *Tri-County Times*, October 22, 2002.

———. "Riggs Home, circa 1856, Is Restored." *Tri-County Times*, June 25, 1984.

Troppens, Anna. "Old Fire Hall Rich in History: Michigan Brewing Company to Transform Historic Structure into Brewery/Restaurant." *Tri-County Times*, February 16, 2011. https://www.tctimes.com/news/local_news/old-fire-hall-rich-in-history/article_8031d69b-c7fc-5241-b38e-66a263aff532.html.

Van Kuren, D. "A Talking House?" *Fenton Independent*, n.d.

Van Leuven, B. "The Spirit of Fenton." *Tri County Times*, February 20, 1998.

Online

Atkins, Thomas Astley. "William Matthew Fenton." Find a Grave. September 23, 2008. https://www.findagrave.com/memorial/30028530/william-matthew-fenton.

City of Fenton. "History of Fenton." https://www.cityoffenton.org/169/History-Of-Fenton

———. "In the Beginning—1869 to 1889." www.cityoffenton.org/266/In-the-Beginning---1869-to-1889.

———. "Tax Assessor." https://www.cityoffenton.org/239/Tax-Information.

8nuts Mothergoose. "Horton-Colwell Opera House—Crossroads Village—Flint, MI—Relocated Structures on Waymarking.com." November 29, 2015. https://www.tctimes.com/living/local-train-depots-were-once-hubs-of-activity/article_93c35820-4dc4-11e5-9b3a-678b8f26e138.html.

Find a Grave. "Oakwood Cemetery." https://www.findagrave.com/cemetery/1290/Oakwood-Cemetery

———. "Oakwood Cemetery: Andrew Jackson Phillips." October 17, 2010. https://www.findagrave.com/memorial/60244911/andrew-j-phillips.

———. "Oakwood Cemetery: Betsy Jane Cheney." November 2, 2008. https://www.findagrave.com/memorial/31074390/betsey-jane-cheney.

———. "Oakwood Cemetery: Bryson Dexter Horton." September 10, 2010. https://www.findagrave.com/memorial/58594282/bryson-dexter-horton.

———. "Shoemaker Cemetery Emily Steere St. Amand." June 30, 2012. https://www.findagrave.com/memorial/92828775/emily-st_amand.

Genesee County Parks and Recreation. "Colwell Opera House." https://geneseecountyparks.org/crossroads-village/attractions/colwell-opera-house/.

Genesee-Oakland-Livingston County MI Biographies. "Chapman Brothers, (1892): Waite, Elihu 1830." www.files.usgwarchives.net/mi/genesee/bios/waite772gbs.txt.

George N. Fuller Lewis Publishing Company. "The Underground Railroad in Michigan." Genealogy Trails. 1939. https://genealogytrails.com/mich/underground.html.

Hinterman, Peter. "The History of Genesee County Cities: Part 3: Fenton Settled: 1834." *My City Magazine*, March 2, 2020. http://www.mycitymag.com/the-history-of-genesee-county-cities-part-three-fenton-settled-1834/.

Holice, Deb, and Clayton Holice. "The History of Genesee County, MI, Chapter V, Fenton Township." USGenNet. June 1, 2002. http://www.usgennet.org/usa/mi/county/lapeer/gen/ch5/fenton.html.

Library of Congress. "Sanborn Fire Maps, (1880–1909)." www.loc.gov/item/sanborn04006_003/.

Michigan Living. "7 Historic Homes in Fenton, Michigan." Michigan Houses Online. February 12, 2019. https://www.michiganhousesonline.com/7-historic-homes-in-fenton-michigan/.

M., Nancy. "Osbert Edwin 'Bert' Williams Jr." Find a Grave, September 20, 2013. https://www.findagrave.com/memorial/117373891/osbert-edwin-williams.

Nationwide Children's Organization. "Asperger's Syndrome." https://www.nationwidechildrens.org/conditions/aspergers-syndrome.

Robinson, John. "Haunted Michigan: Paranormal Activity at the Fenton Hotel." June 15, 2018. https://99wfmk.com/thefentonhotel2018/.

Rynearson, J. "Bryson Horton's Estate Is Not Great Lakes National Cemetery." https://www.tctimes.com/bryson-hortons-estate-is-now-great-lakes-national-cemetery/article_cf72ad4a-4aa2-59f5-9893-f7b52cc7151a.html.

———. "What Was Happening in Fenton—January 1892." February 11, 2009. https://www.tctimes.com/news/local_news/what-was-happening-in-fenton-january-1892/article_6c229265-ccb8-54ee-a9de-77129ebef2a5.html.

Stegall, Yvonne, and Tim Jagielo. "Crossroads Village—Historical Buildings, Holiday Lights." December 10, 2014. https://www.tctimes.com/living/crossroads-village-historical-buildings-holiday-lights/article_c1dcd5d2-807a-11e4-a9f8-279389356e82.html.

Van Horn, Ed. "1892 Portrait & Biographical Album of Genesee, Lapeer & Tuscola Counties, Chapman Bros. (211–17)." USGenNet. October 24, 1999. www.usgennet.org/usa/mi/county/tuscola/book/book211-218.htm.

Weird Universe. "Joe Smallbone, Eccentric." October 18, 2015. http://www.weirduniverse.net/blog/comments/joe_smallbone_eccentric/.

Wikipedia. "Cynthia Roberts Gorton." https://en.wikipedia.org/wiki/Cynthia_Roberts_Gorton.

———. "Square D." https://en.wikipedia.org/wiki/Square_D.

Wood, Edwin O. "History of Genesee County, Michigan, Her People, Industries and Institutions." USGenNet. 1916. www.usgennet.org/use/mi/county/lapeer/gen/ch5/fenton.html.

Video

Blinderman, Ilia. "Thomas Edison and His Trusty Kinetoscope Create the Frist Movie Filed in the U.S. (c. 1889)." Open Culture. March 25, 2014. https://www.openculture.com/2014/03/thomas-edison-and-kinetoscope-create-the-first-movie-filmed-in-the-us-c-1889.html.

DanOCan. "How a Grain Elevator Works and Why I Think They Are Amazing Structures." YouTube. August 9, 2021. https://www.youtube.com/watch?v=E7YqMo6zW5w.

Rescue Techs LLC. "Working Grain Elevator Demo." YouTube. June 3, 2018. https://www.youtube.com/watch?v=Q743aBG9vaI.

Whitehurst, Bonnie. "Joe Smallbones." YouTube. October 12, 2015. https://www.youtube.com/watch?v=XqcjP1UOsig.

ABOUT THE AUTHOR

Brenda Hasse is a multi-award-winning author who writes in various genres, both fiction and nonfiction. A resident of Fenton, Michigan, she has researched the city's history and created scripts for the Fenton Village Players and other volunteers to perform during the Fenton Historic Ghost Walks and the Historical Fenton Cemetery Walk. In 2022, Brenda published *The Haunted Tours of Fenton*, highlighting the tours throughout the city, Fenton's history and hauntings, and the scripts and spooky jokes performed by the tour guides. Through conference speaking engagements, Brenda shares her knowledge of writing and publishing with others. With her cats, Petey and Max, by her side and the love and support of her husband, Charles, she continues to create fascinating works of fiction and nonfiction.

FREE eBOOK OFFER

Scan the QR code below, enter your e-mail address and get our original Haunted America compilation eBook delivered straight to your inbox for free.

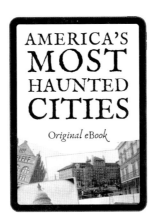

ABOUT THE BOOK

Every city, town, parish, community and school has their own paranormal history. Whether they are spirits caught in the Bardo, ancestors checking on their descendants, restless souls sending a message or simply spectral troublemakers, ghosts have been part of the human tradition from the beginning of time.

In this book, we feature a collection of stories from five of America's most haunted cities: Baltimore, Chicago, Galveston, New Orleans and Washington, D.C.

SCAN TO GET
AMERICA'S MOST HAUNTED CITIES

Having trouble scanning? Go to:
biz.arcadiapublishing.com/americas-most-haunted-cities

Visit us at
www.historypress.com